Analyzing Single System Design Data

POCKET GUIDES TO
SOCIAL WORK RESEARCH METHODS

Series Editor
Tony Tripodi, DSW
Professor Emeritus, Ohio State University

WILLIAM R. NUGENT

Analyzing Single System Design Data

OXFORD
UNIVERSITY PRESS

2010

OXFORD

UNIVERSITY PRESS

Oxford University Press, Inc., publishes works that further
Oxford University's objective of excellence
in research, scholarship, and education.

Oxford   New York
Auckland   Cape Town   Dar es Salaam   Hong Kong   Karachi
Kuala Lumpur   Madrid   Melbourne   Mexico City   Nairobi
New Delhi   Shanghai   Taipei   Toronto

With offices in
Argentina   Austria   Brazil   Chile   Czech Republic   France   Greece
Guatemala   Hungary   Italy   Japan   Poland   Portugal   Singapore
South Korea   Switzerland   Thailand   Turkey   Ukraine   Vietnam

Published by Oxford University Press, Inc.
198 Madison Avenue, New York, New York 10016

www.oup.com

Oxford is a registered trademark of Oxford University Press.

Library of Congress Cataloging-in-Publication Data

Nugent, William R.
Analyzing single system design data / William R. Nugent.
p.   cm.
Includes bibliographical references and index.
ISBN 978-0-19-536962-5
1. Social sciences—Statistical methods.   I. Title.
HA29.N825 2009
519.5—dc22
2009013839

1   3   5   7   9   8   6   4   2

Printed in the United States of America
on acid-free paper

Contents

Introduction

T his book is about the analysis of data from what have been called single case designs; single subject designs; single system designs; intrasubject research designs; and $n = 1$ designs by various writers (e.g., Barlow, Hayes, & Nelson, 1984; Barlow & Hersen, 1984; Bloom, Fischer, & Orme, 2008; Kazdin, 1982; Kratochwill, 1992; Nugent, Sieppert, & Hudson, 2001). The most commonly used approach to analyzing single case design data is visual analysis (e.g., Franklin, Gorman, Beasley, & Allison, 1996; Gibson, 1988; Kazdin, 1982; Parsonson & Baer, 1986, 1992). When conducting a visual analysis, the researcher or practitioner inspects graphed data and looks for clear and obvious changes in data patterns across phases (Barlow et al., 1984; Bloom et al., 1999; Franklin et al., 1996; Kazdin, 1982; Parsonson & Baer, 1986). The rules governing the visual analysis of single case data are subjective, and proponents of these methods view this subjectivity as a strength (e.g., Parsonson & Baer, 1992). Advocates of visual analysis have argued that unaided visual analysis methods essentially are low power; hence, only the largest and most practically relevant effects are found (e.g., Baer, 1977; Michael, 1974; Nourbakhsh & Ottenbacher, 1994; Parsonson & Baer, 1986). In this sense visual methods lead to conservative tests of intervention effects, where small effects cannot be discerned: If the effect is not big enough to be obvious, it is not worth seeing anyway.

Research on visual analysis procedures, however, has led to a number of criticisms of this approach to analyzing single case data (Rubin & Knox, 1996). For example, numerous researchers have found low rates of agreement across persons conducting visual analyses of graphed single case design data and have raised questions about both type I and type II error rates associated with visual analyses (e.g., Bailey, 1984; Boykin & Nelson, 1981; DeProspero & Cohen, 1979; Furlong & Wampold, 1981, 1982; Gibson & Ottenbacher, 1988; Harbst, Ottenbacher, & Harris, 1991; Matyas & Greenwood, 1990; Ottenbacher, 1990; Ottenbacher & Cusick, 1991).

These problems with visual analysis methods have led many to advocate the use of statistical methods for analyzing single case design data (e.g., Brossart, Parker, Olson, & Mahadevan, 2006; Busk & Marascuilo, 1992; Campbell, 2004; Crosbie, 1995; Gentile, Roden, & Klein, 1974; Orme & Cox, 2001; Stocks & Williams, 1995), and research has been done comparing visual and statistical methods of data analysis (e.g., Jones, Weinrott, & Vaught, 1978; Nourbakhsh & Ottenbacher, 1994; Stocks & Williams, 1995), though the actual use of statistical analysis in single case methodology is rare and remains controversial (e.g., Huitema, 1985, 1986, 1988; McCleary & Welsh, 1992). Numerous statistical procedures have been proposed for analyzing single case design data, including analysis of variance procedures (Gentile, Roden, & Klein, 1974); regression methods (Gresham & Noell, 1993); the C-statistic (Tryon, 1982); the two-standard deviation band approach (Gottman & Leiblum, 1974); celeration (trend line) plus binomial test (White and Haring, 1980); interrupted time series analysis (Gottman, 1981); methods based on statistical process control (Nugent, 2000; Orme & Cox, 2001); regression-discontinuity methods (Stocks & Williams, 1995); median-based graphical methods (Parker & Hagan-Burke, 2007); as well as a variety of other approaches (Brossart et al., 2006; Campbell, 2004; Crosbie, 1987; Edington, 1982; Wolery & Billingsley, 1982).

Some have investigated the use of graphical visual aids for addressing problems with the visual analysis of single case design data. Perhaps most notable among these visual aids is the use of any of a number of methods for visually representing phase trend (Bailey, 1984; Hojem & Ottenbacher, 1988; Johnson & Ottenbacher, 1991; Nourbakhsh & Ottenbacher, 1994; Nugent, 2000; Ottenbacher & Cusick, 1991; Rojahn & Schutze, 1985; White & Haring, 1980). Methods have also been developed that are based on phase mean and median lines (e.g., Hsen-Hsing, 2006; Ma, 2006; Parker & Hagan-Burke, 2007). The results of much of this research has suggested that the use of these aids may improve on the interrater agreement concerning the presence or absence of change, though not all studies have led to this conclusion (e.g., Normand & Bailey, 2006).

ORGANIZATION OF THIS BOOK

This book is meant to be a "pocket book," and hence relatively brief. Because of this, the breadth of topics in the analysis of single case design data that could be covered is truncated. I make no claims whatsoever that the material covered in this book is exhaustive of the subject matter. An exhaustive consideration of the issues touched upon here would require a much longer book, well beyond a "pocket book," so I necessarily have had to make choices about issues that would, and would not, be covered. The choices made were mine alone and any criticisms should be directed towards me. The depth to which I have considered the topics in this book is also, necessarily, rather limited. I therefore also make no claim that the material discussed here is as detailed as it could be. A treatment that is both exhaustive and detailed would require a much longer book. I therefore apologize to any readers who find that a topic that he or she considers important is either not covered in sufficient depth or not covered at all.

This book was written primarily for doctoral students and researchers. It is not intended as a primary text for master's-level students in, say, a practice evaluation course. Thus, the book in my thinking could serve as a primary text in a doctoral-level research, practice evaluation, program evaluation, or data analysis course. It could also serve as a collateral text in a Ph.D.-level research, practice evaluation, program evaluation, or data analysis course. If the book were to be used in a master's-level course, it would, in my view, be best used as an auxiliary text, with students reading selected chapters and/or portions of chapters.

I do a brief overview of the logic of single case design methodology, and of more common single case designs, in Chapter 1. This is not an exhaustive treatment, and I assume that the reader has at least a basic understanding of research methodology. The level of knowledge I assume is what would be obtained from a foundation course on research methods. The reader should be somewhat familiar with the issues of *internal* and *external validity* in single case design methodology since this is material I do not cover in the book. If the instructor using this book has reason to believe that students are lacking in their understanding of the concepts of internal and external validity, I recommend for Ph.D. students the general explication of these concepts in Chapter 2 of, and in particular the explication of these issues in interrupted time series designs in Chapter 5 of, Cook and Campbell (1979). For master's or baccalaureate students I recommend the treatment of these issues by Bloom, Fischer, and Orme (2008) or Rubin and Babbie (2007). The reader is also expected to have a basic knowledge of statistical concepts, such as of the mean and median, the notion of variability, and that of a "least squares regression line." This latter concept could be introduced in a lecture as needed. Chapter 1 should be easily readable by doctoral-level students, and by master's- or baccalaureate-level students who have the prerequisite knowledge identified previously.

There is no way around it: Chapter 2 is, as a friend of mine would say, most likely a "real bear." This chapter is for doctoral students and researchers. In Chapter 2 I focus on regression-discontinuity statistical models, and on the so-called ARIMA models for analyzing interrupted time series designs. To many of you, this advanced data analysis topic is placed too early in the book. This was certainly the view of some of those who reviewed early drafts of the book. Some reviewers even suggested that the topic should not be covered in the book. I have, nonetheless, chosen not only to cover this analysis methodology, but also to place it early in the book. I do this so that I can emphasize several issues that are important in the analysis of single case design data in ways that I could not do otherwise. The ARIMA models are in many ways, at least to my thinking, paradigmatic of interrupted time series analysis. Covering this data analysis approach will enable me to introduce the reader to important analysis issues that he or she can keep in mind as various statistical and graphical analysis procedures are subsequently covered. Especially important are the notions of autocorrelation in time series data (Huitema, 1988), the various forms of autocorrelational structure that can be found in time series data, and the need for substantial amounts of data to adequately model autocorrelation.

Another important issue in the analysis of single subject data emphasized in this chapter is the problem caused by the very small numbers of observations in the phases of most such studies. An understanding of the process of identifying and modeling the structure of autocorrelation in a time series can sensitize the reader to the perhaps intractable problem of analyzing the very short interrupted time series characteristically seen in single case research designs. A related issue of concern with very short interrupted time series is the very challenging need to find a way to rule out chance variation as an explanation for the variability seen in phases, and the attendant risk of overinterpreting random variation as meaningful trends. With the ARIMA methodology covered in Chapter 2, the reader will have available conceptual resources that will enable him or her to consider the analysis of brief time series, using either visual, graphical, or statistical methods, with greater sophistication and complexity than if the ARIMA methods appeared later in the book, or not at all.

In Chapter 2 I assume the reader has had a course on multiple regression analysis. This makes this chapter most appropriate for Ph.D.-level students and of course for fellow researchers. This chapter might be used as collateral reading in a course on interrupted time series analysis, or as a primary text in an advanced data analysis seminar in which interrupted time series analysis is covered. The section of the chapter in which I discuss the problem of autocorrelation should be readable by master's-level students who are familiar with the correlation coefficient and who receive appropriate support from the course instructor. I would suggest that master's-level students read this section of the chapter and then skip the remainder. This can be done, I believe, without any loss of continuity in the subject matter.

Chapter 3 focuses on the analysis of single case design data using graphical, statistical, and a combination of graphical and statistical methods. The use of lines drawn into phases to represent the central tendency of the data in the phase, the trend of the data in the phase, and the variability of the data in the phase are all considered and illustrated. Several methods of representing the "background variability" of the data relative to the phase mean and relative to a linear representation of the phase trend are considered and illustrated. No-trend and trend-based methodologies for making inferences about change are also considered and illustrated. I assume an understanding of simple linear regression, as well as of simple statistical notions such as the mean, median, and indices of variability, such as the standard deviation. This chapter should be accessible to Ph.D.-, and with appropriate support master's-level students. The technical proofs in this chapter can be skipped, if desired, with no loss of continuity. These proofs are for doctoral students and fellow researchers.

Chapter 4 describes methods for integrating single case design and group comparison methodologies. This chapter assumes knowledge of multiple regression analysis. This chapter is for Ph.D.-level students and researchers. The use of multilevel models, such as the hierarchical linear models described by Bryk and Raudenbush (1992), are discussed and illustrated using data from two studies that combined group comparison and single case methods. One of these examples involves a linear representation of trends in the single case designs. A second example illustrates a quadratic representation of trends across phases of the single case design elements. This chapter could serve as auxiliary reading for students taking a course on hierarchical linear models, or as primary reading in an advanced data analysis course covering this topic. This is not a chapter for master's-level students.

In Chapter 5 I make a series of recommendations for analyzing single subject data and of areas for future research and development. These include methods for better representing background variability from a baseline phase projected into and across an adjacent treatment phase; suggested revisions in decision rules from statistical process control (SPC) methodology; and suggestions for making more explicit what may be hidden and implicit assumptions made by those who conduct purely visual analyses, without any aids, of single case design data. I also use a simulated 50-data point time series to try to illustrate and further emphasize how easy it is to misinterpret random variation as a meaningful "signal." This chapter should be readable by both master's- and doctoral-level students. My hope is that this chapter can serve as a starting point for lively discussion and debate about the analysis of single case design data, as well as a source for new research and development in this area.

ACKNOWLEDGMENTS

I could not have written this book without the presence in my life of numerous people. First, of course, are my parents, William J. Nugent and Mary Margaret Nugent, both of whom passed away recently. My mother, in fact, died while I was writing this Introduction (February 27, 2009). Both of my parents sacrificed greatly to ensure that I finished college and then went to graduate school. I will always be grateful for these sacrifices. Then, of course, there is Dr. Walter W. Hudson, also recently deceased, who was, and who remains, an inspiration to me in so many ways. I will always admire Walt's ability to so eloquently express his ideas to a group of colleagues. There are many other people who have been, and who continue to be, sources of inspiration in my continued education. These are too many to list, and I hesitate to even try out of fear that I will leave out someone important to me.

I also need to acknowledge the support of my wife, Jan Hankins, who has had to endure many hours with me sitting at the computer writing—and then rewriting—this book. Jan has also helped with this writing, for example, by "proofing" various portions, checking references, and providing other assistance. I thank her profoundly. I also want to acknowledge the support given to me by the many companion animals who have accompanied me through the years. Many of them have played "tug-of-rope" near me, slept (snoring loudly) near my feet, or laid with their head on my lap as I worked on this book, providing support by their mere presence. I especially mention two who died while I completed the book: Maya, a Great Dane (August 7, 2008), and Fenris, a wonderful Irish Wolfhound (October 27, 2008). I miss them both too much to convey in words. Finally, I thank the fine people at Oxford University Press for both the opportunity to write this little book and for their tremendous assistance.

William R. Nugent
June 9, 2009

Analyzing Single System Design Data

1

An Overview of Single Case Design Methodology

T he basic logic of single case design methodology is quite simple. A dependent variable, such as a measure of a client's problem or a target of change in an organization, is measured repeatedly across time. These repeated measures are made under differing conditions—or *phases*—and then comparisons made. Single case designs are a form of interrupted time series methodology but with a small number of data points (Cook & Campbell, 1979). Single case designs are built upon two different types of phases: baseline phases and treatment phases (Barlow & Hersen, 1984; Bloom, Fischer, & Orme, 2008; Kazdin, 1982).

BASELINE PHASES

In single case design methodology, repeated measures are made of the dependent variable across a period of time prior to starting an intervention or program intended to induce change. This pretreatment period of observation is referred to as a *baseline phase*, and is generally symbolized with the capital letter *A*. The purpose of the baseline phase is to obtain a longitudinal profile of the dependent variable in the absence of any intervention or treatment (Barlow & Hersen, 1984; Bloom et al., 2008;

Kazdin, 1982). Such a pretreatment time series allows the researcher or evaluator to look for trends—systematic patterns of change in the time series—that might be indicative of historical or maturational factors, as well as patterns suggestive of regression to the mean effects. It also enables the data analyst to model characteristics of the time series prior to a treatment or intervention being applied. This model of baseline phase data patterns serves as the basis of comparison against which data from a subsequent treatment phase are compared. This baseline model is important since an intervention can affect a time series in many ways, as will be seen later (Cook & Campbell, 1979).

An example of a 6-day baseline phase is shown in Figure 1.1 from a single case design evaluation of the treatment of a client's problem with panic attacks reported by Nugent (1993). The day of the week is represented on the horizontal axis, while the severity of the client's problem with panic is represented on the vertical axis. The across-time data on this client's problem with panic shown in this figure illustrate how a baseline phase provides a profile of a problem behavior in the absence of intervention. As will be discussed later, a limitation of a

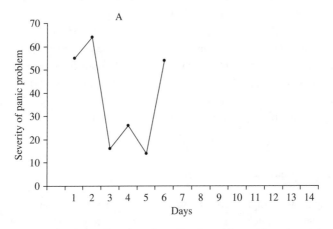

Figure 1.1 Example of a baseline phase for a client's problem with panic attacks. Reproduced with permission of Taylor Francis Group (http://www. informaworld.com), from Nugent, W. (1993). A series of single case design clinical evaluations of an Ericksonian hypnotic intervention used with clinical anxiety. *Journal of Social Service Research, 17*(3/4), 41–69.

baseline such as that in Figure 1.1 is that it is quite short. The small number of observations in this baseline is a characteristic of many single case designs, a trait that makes it difficult to identify many types of patterns that appear in time series data (Cook & Campbell, 1979).

TREATMENT PHASES

In a single case design, the repeated measures are continued during the implementation of an intervention or program. A set of repeated measures obtained during the implementation of a treatment or program is referred to as a *treatment phase* and is generally symbolized by the capital letter *B*. The purpose of the treatment phase is the gathering of a longitudinal profile of the dependent variable during the implementation of some intervention or program intended to impact the dependent variable. *The adjacent treatment and baseline time series are then compared to make inferences about change.* This is the basic logic of the single case design: comparing longitudinal patterns between adjacent phases, usually baseline and treatment phases (Barlow & Hersen, 1984; Kazdin, 1982). The *interruption* of the baseline time series by the implementation of an intervention or program is why single case designs are a type of the aptly named *interrupted time series design*. Indeed, the single case designs described in many texts, such as Kazdin (1982) and Bloom et al. (2008), might be defined as brief interrupted time series designs.

An example of a treatment phase is shown in Figure 1.2. The treatment phase, from Nugent (1993) and labeled as B, is shown adjacent to the baseline phase from Figure 1.1. This figure illustrates three important concepts in single case design methodology: (*1*) the baseline phase provides a profile of the client's problem with panic prior to, and in the absence of, treatment; (*2*) the treatment phase provides a profile of the client's panic problem during the implementation of an intervention; and (*3*) the placement of these two phases immediately adjacent to one another allows a comparison of patterns in the two phases for purposes of determining whether there is a change in the client's problem with panic (Kazdin, 1982).

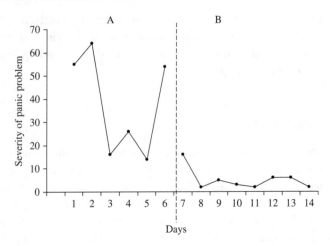

Figure 1.2 Example of a treatment phase adjacent to a baseline phase in a study of the treatment of a problem with panic attacks from Nugent (1993). Reproduced with permission of Taylor Francis Group (http://www.informaworld.com), from Nugent, W. (1993). A series of single case design clinical evaluations of an Ericksonian hypnotic intervention used with clinical anxiety. *Journal of Social Service Research*, *17*(3/4), 41–69.

SOME BASIC SINGLE CASE DESIGNS

B Designs

Probably the simplest single case design to use, and the one most congenial with the provision of professional services, such as counseling and psychotherapy, is the *B design*, in which repeated measures are taken of a client's problem while he or she is receiving services (Nugent, Sieppert, & Hudson, 2001). For example, suppose that a client is being treated by a social worker for depression that is so intense that the client is contemplating suicide. The social worker could use a B design to monitor her or his client's progress, or lack thereof, simply by obtaining weekly measures of her or his client's levels of depression and suicidal thinking, starting with the first meeting. The purpose of the B design, in this case, would be to evaluate whether the client is improving during service provision (Bloom et al., 2008; Nugent et al., 2001). The B design could NOT be used to answer *causal* questions about the impact of the services

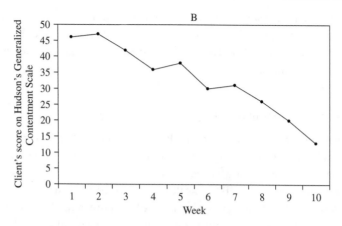

Figure 1.3 Hypothetical B design used to evaluate how a client is doing during the provision of services for depression.

provided by the social worker, such as, "Did the services provided *cause* the client to improve?" Figure 1.3 shows hypothetical data from a B design used to monitor the level of a client's problem with depression during treatment intended to decrease this depression. Since scores on the measure used in this hypothetical B design, the Hudson's Generalized Contentment Scale (GCS; Hudson, 1982), are such that higher scores are indicative of higher levels of depression, and vice versa, the short time series in this B design clearly suggests that the client's depression is decreasing during the 10 weeks of treatment.

AB Designs

The *AB design* has been referred to by some as the "basic" single case design because it makes use of a baseline phase immediately followed by a treatment phase (e.g., Bloom et al., 2008). As already noted, the baseline time series provides a profile of the temporal patterns in the dependent variable in the absence of any intervention. The baseline data patterns are then compared and contrasted against those in the treatment phase to make inferences about (*1*) change and, possibly, (*2*) whether the intervention caused changes in the dependent variable. The chapters in this book focus on the first of these types of inferences.

Design characteristics that allow inferences about causality have been discussed in depth by numerous other authors (e.g., Barlow & Hersen, 1984; Bloom et al., 2008; Kazdin, 1981, 1982). The single case design in Figure 1.2 is an example of an AB design.

Successive Treatments Design

A variation on the theme of an AB design is an *A-B1-B2*, or form of *successive treatments*, design (Bloom et al., 2008). In this design the B1 label indicates that a particular treatment is used during this first treatment phase, while B2 indicates that a different treatment is used during a second treatment phase. Figure 1.4 shows an A-B1-B2-B3-B2 successive treatments design from a study by Nugent (1993). The B1 phase designated the implementation of a hypnotic intervention used to

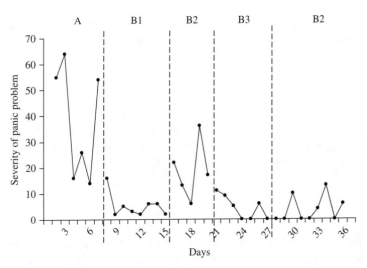

Figure 1.4 An example of an A-B1-B2-B3-B2 design. The dependent variable was a measure of the overall severity of a problem with panic attacks. The intervention used in the B1 phase was a hypnotic induction; in the B2 phase a cognitive-behavioral package; and in the B3 phase a combination of hypnosis and the cognitive-behavioral package. Reproduced with permission of Taylor Francis Group (http://www.informaworld.com), from Nugent, W. (1993). A series of single case design clinical evaluations of an Ericksonian hypnotic intervention used with clinical anxiety. *Journal of Social Service Research, 17*(3/4), 41–69.

reduce the severity of a client's problem with panic attacks. The B2 phase involved the use of a cognitive-behavioral treatment package, and B3 was the combination of the hypnosis and the cognitive-behavioral intervention package.

ABAB Designs

From an internal validity perspective, the *ABAB design* is among the strongest of single case designs in that it can be used to make inferences not only about change, but also about causality. The ABAB design has an initial baseline phase, followed by a treatment phase. Assuming that the intervention or program being studied can, in a very real sense, be withdrawn or stopped, this treatment phase is followed by a second baseline phase. The purpose of this termination of the intervention is to ascertain whether the patterns in the dependent variable revert back, during the second baseline phase, to what they were during the first baseline phase. This second baseline phase is then followed by a second treatment phase during which the intervention or program is reinstated. The purpose is to determine whether the patterns in the dependent variable now return to what they were during the first treatment phase. This alternation of baseline and treatment phases allows the researcher to control many threats to internal validity and make a case that it is the treatment or program that causes the observed changes (Barlow & Hersen, 1984; Bloom et al., 2008; Kazdin, 1982).

An example of an ABAB design is shown in Figure 1.5. This is from a study reported by Heard and Watson (1999). In this study Heard and Watson investigated the use of differential reinforcement (Spiegler & Guevremont, 2003) for reducing the wandering behavior of persons with dementia. The A phases show the percentage of time intervals "Anna" was wandering in the absence of any intervention. In contrast, the B phases show the percentage of time intervals she was wandering while the differential reinforcement of her behavior was in effect.

The logic of this particular investigation was as follows. The first baseline provided a longitudinal profile of "Anna's" wandering behavior prior to implementing the differential reinforcement intervention. The first treatment phase provided a similar profile, but one showing her wandering behavior after the differential reinforcement of her behavior had been implemented. As can be seen in Figure 1.5, the percentage of

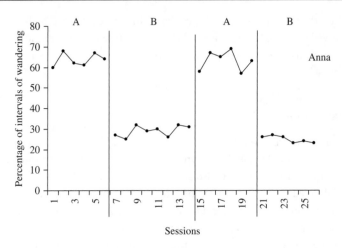

Figure 1.5 An example of an ABAB single case design from Heard and Watson (1999). Reproduced with kind permission of *Journal of Applied Behavior Analysis*. Heard, K., & Watson, T. (1999). Reducing wandering by persons with dementia using differential reinforcement. *Journal of Applied Behavior Analysis*, *32*, 381–384.

time intervals during which Anna wandered decreased dramatically upon implementation of the differential reinforcement of her behavior, and remained at a much lower level across the sessions in which the intervention was implemented. This decrease in percentage of time intervals during which Anna wandered contrasted with the baseline profile in such a manner as to unambiguously suggest that her wandering behavior had decreased under the influence of the intervention. Now, if the intervention was the cause of this change, then the cessation of the intervention in a second baseline phase should see her wandering behavior revert to what it was during the first baseline phase. The data in the second baseline in Figure 1.5 unequivocally suggests this to be the case. Further, if the intervention was the cause of the change in her wandering behavior, then reimplementing the intervention should see this behavior again decrease. The data in Figure 1.5 unmistakably suggest this to be the case.

Overall, Anna's wandering (*1*) decreased relative to the preintervention pattern upon implementing differential reinforcement, (*2*) increased back to preintervention patterns upon stopping the intervention, and then (*3*) decreased again upon reimplementing differential reinforcement. These patterns were clearly consistent with the intervention causing a decrease in Anna's wandering behavior.

B1-B2-B1-B2 Designs

A design similar to the ABAB is the *B1-B2-B1-B2 design*. This design differs from the ABAB in that (*1*) there are no baseline phases and (*2*) the purpose is to compare the relative efficacy of two different treatments, symbolized by the designations B1 and B2. An example of this design was used by Nugent (1992) and illustrated in Figure 1.6. In Nugent's (1992) study, the affective impact of various forms of verbal statements, and verbal responses to client statements, was investigated in a series of simulations. The verbal statements and responses to client statements used by a social worker in a simulated interview during the B1 phases were what Nugent (1992) termed "obstructive" responses. In contrast, the verbal statements and responses to client statements used by the social worker in the simulated interview during the B2 phases were termed "facilitative." The dependent variable in this study was the

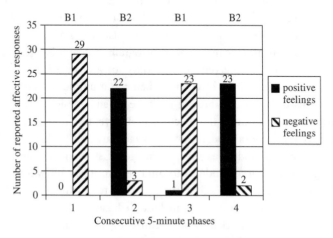

Figure 1.6 An example of a B1-B2-B1-B2 single case design adapted from Nugent (1992). Reproduced from Nugent, W. (1992). The affective impact of a clinical social worker's interviewing style: A series of single case experiments. *Research on Social Work Practice*, *2*(1), 6–27.

report of a participant's emotional reactions to the verbal statements made by the person playing the social worker in the simulated interview.

Note that during the first B1 phase, when the social worker made only "obstructive" types of statements and verbal responses to the person in the client role, participants reported 29 negative emotional responses as opposed to no positive emotional responses. In contrast, during the first B2 phase, when only "facilitative" types of statements and verbal responses were made by the social worker, there were 22 positive emotional responses versus only three negative reactions. Then, during the second B1 phase, there were 23 negative emotional reactions while only a single positive reaction was reported. Finally, during the second B2 phase, there were 23 positive emotional reactions and only two negative. These results were consistent with Nugent's (1992) hypothesis that the "facilitative" verbal style leads to more positive client emotional reactions to a social worker, while the "obstructive" style leads clients to experience more negative emotional responses to a social worker.

Multiple Baseline Designs

The final single case design to be considered here is the *multiple baseline design*, an example of which is shown in Figure 1.7. Use of an ABAB design assumes that it is both ethical and possible to withdraw or stop an intervention. In cases in which it is not ethical and/or impossible to stop an intervention, and the researcher or program evaluator is interested in whether or not an intervention is a *cause* of a change in a problem behavior or other target of change, then the multiple baseline design may be used. Figure 1.7 shows a multiple baseline design across communities used to evaluate the effects of an intervention to reduce the sale of tobacco to minors (Biglan, Ary, & Wagenaar, 2000). The dependent measure in this study was the percentage of stores in a community willing to sell tobacco products to underage youths. This was assessed by having underage youths go to stores and try to buy tobacco products. The intervention being studied included educating merchants, giving "rewards" to store workers who declined to sell tobacco products to underage youths, and positive publicity for merchants and their workers when they refused to sell to underage youths (Biglan et al., 2000, p. 37). The multiple baseline design in Figure 1.7 is called a *multiple baseline (MBL) design across subjects*, and in this case the "subjects" are the

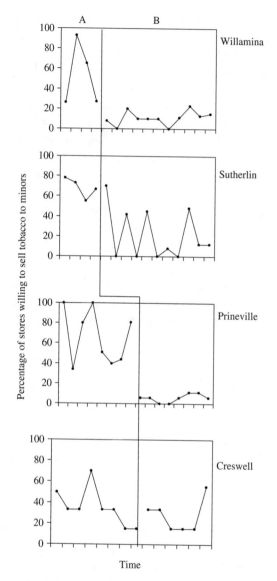

Figure 1.7 Example of multiple baseline design, from Biglan, Ary, and Wagenaar (2000). Reproduced with kind permission from Springer Science + Business Media. Biglan, A., Ary, D., & Wagenaar, A. (2000). The value of interrupted time-series experiments for community intervention research. *Prevention Science*, *1*(1), 38, Figure 3.

communities. The "subjects" in an MBL design can be persons, groups, communities, agencies, schools, or any other system.

The heart of the MBL design is the temporal staggering of the start of the intervention across the subjects, a design feature that leads to baseline phases of differing length for the different subjects. If all of the baseline phases show profiles that indicate no improvement prior to the start of the intervention, and then treatment phase data show improvement at (and only at) the point the intervention is implemented, then a case can be made that not only has change occurred, but also that it is the intervention that is causing the change. The MBL design can be thought of as a stacked series of AB designs, with successive AB designs in the stack having sequentially longer baseline phases.

Combination Designs

Sometimes single case designs of different types can be combined into more complex designs. One example from the author's days as a therapist in an outpatient mental health clinic is shown in Figure 1.8. This is an

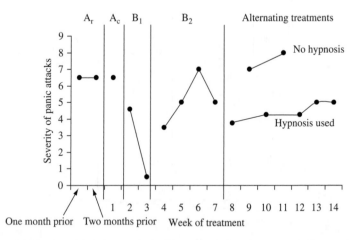

Figure 1.8 An A-B1-B2 design merged with an alternating treatments design. Reproduced with permission of Taylor Francis Group (http://www.informaworld. com), from Nugent, W. (1993). A series of single case design clinical evaluations of an Ericksonian hypnotic intervention used with clinical anxiety. *Journal of Social Service Research*, *17*(3/4), 41–69.

example of an A-B1-B2 design merged with an *alternating treatments design*. This example comes from a single case design evaluation of the treatment of a client suffering from panic attacks. The dependent variable was a 0 (no attacks) to 10 (most severe panic attacks; see Nugent, 1992) measure of the severity of the client's panic attacks. The A_r phase was a *retrospective baseline* (Nugent et al., 2001). In a retrospective baseline, measures of the dependent variable are obtained in the present but represent time points *in the past*, in this case 2 months prior to the start of treatment and 1 month prior to the start of treatment. These measures were obtained by having the client remember back 2 months (and then 1 month) and rate—retrospectively—the severity of the panic attacks. The A_c phase was a *concurrent baseline*; that is, the measures obtained were of the severity of panic attacks at the present time. The single A_c measure was taken during the first session with this client.

In the B1 phase, a combination treatment of hypnosis, cognitive-behavioral therapy (CBT), and pharmacotherapy was implemented. In the B2 phase, the CBT/pharmacotherapy combination was used without the hypnosis. In the alternating treatments portion of the design, the CBT/pharmacotherapy combination was used continuously. There were also weekly sessions during which hypnosis was used in combination with the CBT/pharmacotherapy combination. The measures of the dependent variable made the week after the hypnosis was used together with the CBT/pharmacotherapy combination are identified by the "hypnosis used" label. These data points are connected together showing the cross-time pattern of the client's severity of panic attacks when hypnosis was added to the CBT/pharmacotherapy combination. The measures of the dependent variable made the week after hypnosis was not used are marked in this figure by the "no hypnosis" label and are connected. This across-time profile shows the client's severity of panic attacks during periods when the hypnosis had not been added to the CBT/pharmacotherapy combination. The dual profiles during the alternating treatments portion of this single case design allow for the comparison of two different treatments being implemented during the same phase. As the data in the alternating treatments portion of this figure suggest, the addition of the hypnosis to the CBT/pharmacotherapy combination appeared to enhance the effectiveness of that treatment combination. The alternating treatments design is discussed further in such sources as Bloom et al. (2008).

Other Designs

There are a variety of other single case designs, such as the *multiple baseline across behaviors* and *changing criterion designs*. The reader is referred to sources such as Barlow and Hersen (1984), Kazdin (1982), and Bloom et al. (2008) for detailed discussion of these, as well as other, forms of single case designs.

DATA PATTERNS IN SINGLE CASE DESIGNS

The traditional, and most commonly used, methods for analyzing single case design data are visual approaches. The basic principle of visual analysis can perhaps be best summarized by the sentence, "If you cannot obviously see differences between phases, then any differences that are there are not important enough to be concerned about." The reader is encouraged to look closely again at the data in Figure 1.5. The changes between baseline and treatment phases are visually clear and unarguable, and no statistical analyses are needed to validate these between-phase differences. It is immediately obvious to the naked eye that there are substantial differences between baseline and treatment phases. Advocates of visual analysis methods argue that reliance on visual analysis will lead to the identification of large-magnitude treatment effects, as can be seen in this figure (Baer, 1977). These issues are considered again later.

The analyst using visual methods will look for changes, or contrasts, between phases in terms of (1) level, (2) trend, (3) variability, (4) overlap, and (5) mean. The analyst can also look for (6) the immediacy versus latency of change and (7) the transience versus permanence of change. These forms of contrast will be considered and illustrated using the Prineville data from the Biglan et al. (2000) multiple baseline design shown in Figure 1.7. The Prineville data are shown in Figure 1.9.

Changes in Level

One definition of the term *level* refers to the value of the dependent variable at a given point in time. For example, the dependent variable in the Biglan et al. (2000) study was the percentage of stores willing to sell tobacco products to underage youths. The level of this variable at the

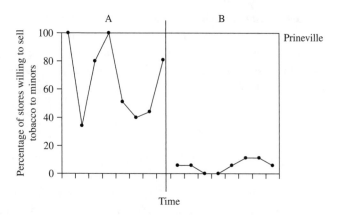

Figure 1.9 Prineville single case design data from Biglan, Ary, and Wagenaar (2000) study.

beginning of baseline for Prineville was 100%. Similarly, the level at the final baseline observation was just above 80%, while at the first treatment phase observation, the level was below 10%. This difference between the last baseline and the first treatment phase observations is one way to define a *change in level* across the A-B phase transition, as is illustrated in Figure 1.10 (other definitions are discussed below).

As is discussed later, this pattern of change across the A-B phase transition also illustrates an *immediate*, or in Cook and Campbell's

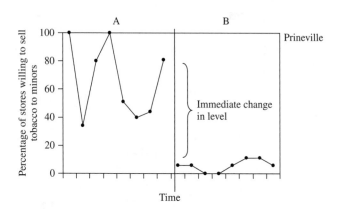

Figure 1.10 Illustration of a change in level across the A-B phase transition. Figure adapted, with permission, from Biglan, Ary, and Wagenaar (2000).

(1979) terms an *instantaneous*, change. The more immediate the change, the more likely it is that the treatment variable was a causal factor in the change (Kazdin, 1981, 1982). Contrariwise, the more delayed the change, the weaker the case is that the independent variable caused the change (Cook & Campbell, 1979; Kazdin, 1981, 1982).

Changes in Trend

Trend refers to how the level of the dependent variable *changes across a phase*. Technically, *trend is the rate of change of the dependent variable*. Trend has also been referred to as *slope* or *drift* (Cook & Campbell, 1979). Visually it appears in a phase as a general tendency for the dependent variable to be increasing (or decreasing) in some systematic manner. Trend can be linear or nonlinear. As will be shown later, the linear trend of the data in a phase can be represented graphically by a line or arrow constructed in one of several ways. The linear trends in baseline and treatment phases are shown in Figure 1.11 by arrows drawn in the phases. The solid arrow in baseline shows the mean baseline phase trend, while the solid arrow in treatment phase shows the mean treatment phase trend. Also shown in this figure is the *change in linear trend between the two*

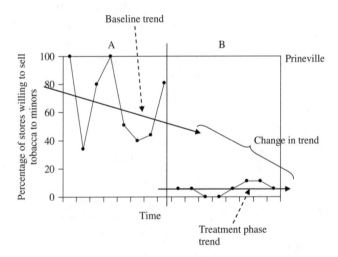

Figure 1.11 Graphic illustration of phase trends (*solid arrows*), and of change in linear trend across phases, using data from Biglan, Ary, and Wagenaar (2000).

phases. The mean baseline linear trend is slightly decreasing, while the mean treatment phase trend is flat, or constant. The change in trend is from a slight decreasing to a constant, or zero, trend.

Changes in Variability

Variability refers to the extent to which the level of the dependent variable fluctuates across the phases of a single case design. There are two types of variability, *systematic* and *nonsystematic*, as illustrated in Figure 1.12. Systematic variation will include variation in the dependent variable due to linear (or nonlinear) trend. It will also include variation that is systematic—that is, variation that is orderly in some fashion—and that is due to the influence of any of a number of relevant factors that may or may not be known. In contrast, nonsystematic variability is random.

As can be seen in Figure 1.12, there is considerable overall variability in level of the dependent variable for Prineville during baseline, with a small amount associated with the small decreasing linear trend, while the

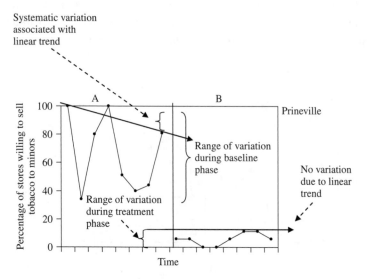

Figure 1.12 Illustration of forms of variation across single case design phases using Prineville data from Biglan, Ary, and Wagenaar (2000).

remainder is unexplained variation relative to—that is, as measured against—this decreasing trend. There is much less variability across treatment phase, none of which is systematic variability that is associated with linear trend.

Degree of Overlap

Single case design analysts also consider *overlap*. The notion of overlap can be explicated using the illustration in Figure 1.13. The ranges of variability across baseline phase, and across treatment phase, are shown in this figure. Note that these ranges of variability for the two phases *do not overlap relative to horizontal lines drawn through the phases*. Thus, there is no overlap between the ranges of variation in the dependent variable for baseline and treatment phases. Had these ranges of variability overlapped, then it would be said that there was overlap in the ranges of values of the dependent variable between baseline and treatment phases. The greater the degree of overlap, the less visually apparent changes between the two phases become. Conversely, the greater the width of the region of nonoverlap, the more visually apparent it is that there is a difference in the data between baseline and treatment phases. The notion of overlap is important in several approaches to

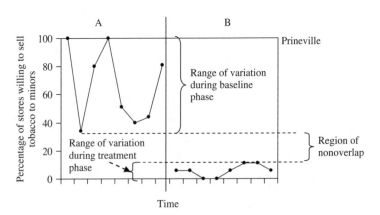

Figure 1.13 Graphic illustration of notion of overlap, based on Prineville data from Biglan, Ary, and Wagenaar (2000).

analyzing single case design data (Barlow, Hayes, & Nelson, 1984; Kazdin, 1982).

Changes in Phase Mean

A *change in means* across two phases refers to the extent to which the mean value of the dependent variable in one phase differs from the mean value for an adjacent phase. This is illustrated in Figure 1.14 for the Prineville data. The flat dashed lines in baseline and treatment phases in this figure show the mean level of the dependent variable. Also shown in this figure is the difference between the phase means, or the change in mean from baseline to treatment phase. The change in means between phases is a second form (and special case) of change in level between phases.

Immediacy of Change

Another pattern that can be used to assess the change from a baseline to a treatment phase, or between two different but adjacent treatment phases, is the *latency of change* (Kazdin, 1982). The latency, or immediacy, of change refers to how immediate versus delayed any change is across the transition from one phase to another. As has already been noted, and can

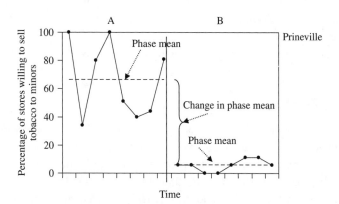

Figure 1.14 Graphic illustration of change in mean between baseline and treatment phase using Prineville data from Biglan, Ary, and Wagenaar (2000).

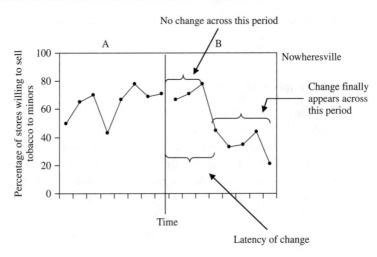

Figure 1.15 Contrived data for hypothetical community called "Nowheresville" showing change between phases that has some degree of latency.

readily be seen, the change in the data patterns from baseline phase to treatment phase in Figure 1.9 for the Prineville data from Biglan et al. (2000) is immediate. There is no latency of change. This is also obvious in the data in Figure 1.5.

Contrast this with the hypothetical data in Figure 1.15. These contrived data are for an imaginary community called "Nowheresville" that was hypothetically investigated as part of a study such as that by Biglan et al. (2000). Note that while there is apparent change from baseline to treatment phase, this change takes some time to appear. In this case, there is some degree of latency of change (Nugent et al., 2001).

Permanent Versus Temporary Change

One other data pattern the analyst will look for is *permanent* versus *temporary change*. A change is permanent if the data patterns suggest that whatever change is observed does not decay or deteriorate across time. If the observed change decays with time, the change is temporary. This is illustrated in Figures 1.16 and 1.17. A temporary change in treatment phase relative to baseline can be seen in Figure 1.16, while Figure 1.17 shows what appears to be a permanent change.

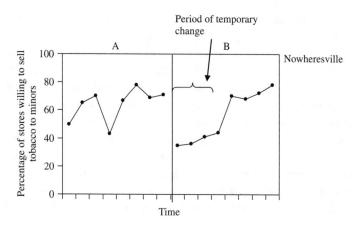

Figure 1.16 Hypothetical data for community called "Nowheresville" showing a temporary change in percentage of stores willing to sell tobacco products to minors.

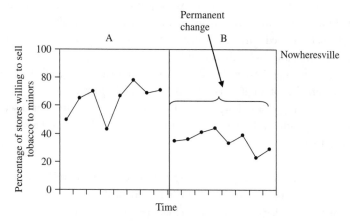

Figure 1.17 Hypothetical data for community called "Nowheresville" showing a permanent change in percentage of stores willing to sell tobacco products to minors.

COMBINATIONS OF CHANGES AND "SIGNIFICANCE"

The visual analyst looks for the foregoing types of contrasts, individually and in combination, between adjacent phases in a single case design. The greater the number and forms of contrasts, and the larger these visually apparent changes are in magnitude, the more convincing the case that can be made that change has occurred between phases. In traditional visual analysis, there is no formal notion of "significance" that is invoked, as there is in tests of statistical significance (see Chow, 1996), when determining if change has occurred. Indeed, tests of statistical significance are *not* traditionally used when analyzing single case design data. Rather, the analyst *uses the data patterns in baseline and projects them into treatment phase as a forecast of what would likely continue to happen if nothing intervened to change the dependent variable.* This is an important precept used in a number of analysis approaches discussed in more detail below. The analyst, in a sense, models the baseline phase data patterns and then uses them to forecast into treatment phase what would occur if there were no change in the baseline time series into and across treatment phase. This methodology is analogous to that from time series analysis in which a statistically modeled time series is used to make forecasts about future realizations of the time series (e.g., Ostrom, 1990). However, unlike the formal statistical methods from time series analysis, the visual analyst makes no use of rigorously defined criteria, for instance, statistical significance, for identifying data patterns, such as trend.

Parsonson and Baer (1986) discussed the issue of "significance" of characteristics of single case design data in the context of the visual analysis of single case design data. They noted (p. 167), in their discussion of hypothetical baseline data on a young girl's safely crossing a street, that:

> A slow increasing trend in her likelihood to cross the street safely can be seen. In a 8-point baseline, that might be attributed to chance variation; on the other hand, it is visible, and interpretation later will depend on what changes can be seen relative to this baseline. Thus, it does not really matter whether the baseline is truly increasing; what matters is that any intervention applied after this baseline must produce effects clearly contrasting to it—and any intervention that cannot produce effects better than that need not be validated as functional, anyway: it will have no use in a pragmatic world.

Thus, *if you cannot see obvious contrasts between adjacent phases—such as baseline and treatment phase data—then important change has not occurred*. If you have to extract a small change between phases from the data using some form of statistical significance testing, then the change is likely to be of little or no practical importance. If it is not visually obvious, it is of little importance, whether it is "statistically significant" or not. This is perhaps the central principle of the traditional visual analysis of single case design data (Baer, 1977; Kazdin, 1982).

This principle has considerable appeal. Arguably any change that is so large that, in a sense, it smacks the analyst in the face will in all likelihood attain statistical significance. The data in Figure 1.5 are again pointed to. For all of its conceptual appeal, however, this principle must be considered within the context of humans' propensity to see patterns where none exists. There is ample research documenting the tendency for human beings to see systematic patterns in random variation (e.g., Gilovich, 1993; Gilovich, Griffin, & Kahneman, 2002; Plous, 1993). This tendency is especially pronounced when the amount of data that are being used to make inferences is small. This can be illustrated in the context of time series analysis using the 30-data point time series in Figure 1.18. This time series was generated by adding a normally distributed random variable with mean of zero and standard deviation of five to a constant level of 30. The dashed horizontal line in this figure shows the constant level of 30, and the variation relative to this constant level is merely random variation. Viewing the entire 30-data point series makes the random nature of this variation about the constant level of 30 more apparent. However, suppose that the four data points, shown

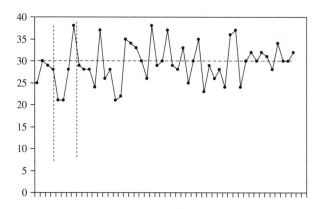

Figure 1.18 A 30-data point time series, with a small local section marked out.

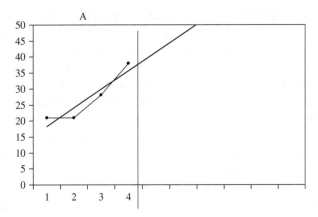

Figure 1.19 Possible four-data point baseline phase abstracted from 30-data point time series in Figure 1.18, with linear trend line drawn in.

between the two vertical dashed lines in Figure 1.18, were observed as a baseline time series *without the data analyst knowing the nature of the longer time series from which these four data points are extracted.* This hypothetical four-data point baseline is shown in Figure 1.19 with an ordinary least squares trend line added. The apparent trend in an increasing direction is obvious, and using Parsonson and Baer's (1986) comments quoted previously as a guide, this apparent increasing trend would be an important basis against which to compare and contrast treatment phase data patterns. However, *the apparent increasing trend is an illusion; it is an erroneous interpretation of random variation that is aided and abetted by the small number of observations, viewed and interpreted outside of the context of the longer time series, in this baseline phase.* This tendency of humans to see patterns in random variation must be neither ignored nor underestimated when analyzing the short time series frequently found in single case designs. This issue will be considered again in later chapters.

Critical Incident Recording

A useful procedure for helping represent the time series data for a particular individual person, group, or system is including on a single case design graph a notation identifying a *critical incident* associated with

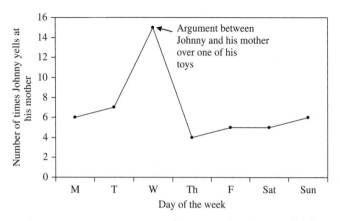

Figure 1.20 Baseline data for Johnny's yelling behavior, with an unusually high level on Wednesday and a critical incident notation.

a particular data point, or series of data points. A critical incident is any event that may be at least partially responsible for the level of the dependent variable at a particular time point, or across a particular time period. For example, suppose that baseline data for the number of times that little Johnny yells as his mother looks as in Figure 1.20. Note the unusually high level, relative to other baseline levels, of the dependent variable on Wednesday. The notation on the graph indicating that there was an argument between Johnny and his mother, about one of his toys, provides a possible explanation for the unusually high frequency of his yelling at his mom on this particular day. This notation is an example of critical incident recording.

ILLUSTRATIVE VISUAL ANALYSIS

Let us now do an illustrative visual analysis. Consider the Prineville data shown in Figure 1.21. The data show several contrasts between baseline and treatment phases. Most notable are (1) the large immediate change in level between baseline and treatment phases, (2) the large differences in the variability in the within-phase data between baseline and treatment phases, (3) the large difference between phase means, and (4) the rather large region of nonoverlap. The data in treatment phase also suggest (5) a permanent change from baseline. While there is a change

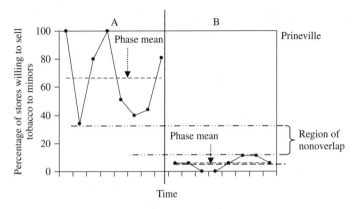

Figure 1.21 Prineville data from Biglan, Ary, and Wagenaar (2000), showing phase means and the region of nonoverlap between baseline and treatment phase ranges of variability.

in trend from a small decreasing trend during baseline to a flat trend during treatment phase, this contrast is not as substantial as are the other differences between phases. This particular change is also abetted by a *floor effect* on the dependent variable; that is, the data cannot go lower than 0%, and the treatment phase data cluster near this floor, so any continued decreasing trend is limited if not impossible. Visually there is a compelling set of differences between the two phases that suggests that there is a change in the percentage of stores willing to sell tobacco products to underage youths between baseline and treatment phases.

In contrast, consider the data for Creswell from the Biglan et al. (2000) study shown in Figure 1.22. Note that there is a visually apparent change in trend across the two phases, but this trend change is due solely to the last treatment phase data point. If this data point were not there, the treatment phase data would also show a decreasing trend. Note further that there is a small difference between phase means, that there is a small difference between the ranges of variability for the two phases, and that the range of baseline phase variability completely overlaps with the treatment phase range of variability. These contrasts between baseline and treatment phases for Creswell make a much less compelling case for change than do the contrasts discussed above for the Prineville data. A plausible alternate hypothesis to that of change between the two phases

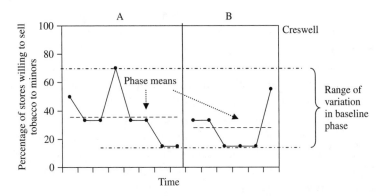

Figure 1.22 Creswell community data from Biglan, Ary, and Wagenaar (2000) study.

for Creswell is that the treatment phase data are nothing more than a continuation of the baseline data patterns. This alternate hypothesis is especially compelling if the baseline phase data patterns are extended into and across the treatment phase as a forecast of what would occur if no change occurred between the two phases.

STRENGTHS AND LIMITATIONS OF VISUAL ANALYSIS

The main strength of visual analysis methods is the probable low power associated with inferences of change. Only the largest and most visually apparent changes will be identified, and these large effects imply clinical and practical relevance (Baer, 1977). This possible advantage must be considered, however, within the context of research that has consistently suggested that visual analysis methods have low interrater reliability (Bailey, 1984; DeProspero & Cohen, 1979; Furlong & Wampold, 1981; Gibson & Ottenbacher, 1988; Harbst, Ottenbacher, & Harris, 1991; Matyas & Greenwood, 1990; Ottenbacher, 1990; Ottenbacher & Cusick, 1991). Low interrater agreement implies poor validity of inferences of change.

This likely low validity of inferences about change is perhaps the most significant limitation of the use of purely visual analysis procedures. A related limitation is that analysts using visual analysis methods almost certainly are doing so within the context of assumptions that are not explicitly articulated by the analyst. In many cases, these silent assumptions may be poorly understood by the analyst and may even be beyond the analyst's awareness. In this latter circumstance, the analysis will be quite vulnerable to confirmation biases, expectations, personal ambitions, and other human characteristics that make for erroneous inferences, whether scientific (see Giere, 1990) or clinical (see Garb, 1998). Especially likely is the erroneous interpretation of random variation as meaningful trends that would support results "desired" or in some manner expected by the analyst (Gilovich, 1993). In the language of signal detection theory, this would be the erroneous interpretation of noise as signal (Brennan, 2001).

2

Regression-Discontinuity and ARIMA Models

T his chapter focuses on what are referred to as regression-discontinuity models and on a special, somewhat advanced form of interrupted time series analysis often referred to as ARIMA models. ARIMA analysis offers, in the author's view, a paradigmatic model of interrupted time series analysis that allows the explication of a number of issues fundamental to the statistical analysis of interrupted time series data. These issues are also relevant to the analysis—visual and statistical—of data from single system designs (see also Busk & Marascuilo, 1992; Crosbie, 1995). Hence, while the statistical methods in this chapter are clearly advanced and arguably better placed in a later chapter (or, perhaps, even omitted from the book completely), this chapter is nevertheless placed here. In this way the reader will be familiar with analysis issues articulated in this chapter as he or she reads later chapters, and can consider the methods discussed in later chapters within the context of the issues raised and considered here. The most significant issues discussed in this chapter are the length of the time series and the identification and adequate modeling of the *autocorrelation* structure of a time series. The important lessons for time series analysis are that (*1*) the autocorrelation of concern is that between residuals from a statistical model fit to the time series; (*2*) autocorrelation can show up in complex patterns; (3) autocorrelation can have substantial and deleterious effects on estimates of sampling variability of parameter estimates and on tests of statistical significance; and (4) it takes a lot of data to adequately identify and model patterns of autocorrelation.

AUTOCORRELATION AND ITS EFFECTS

The term *autocorrelation* generally refers to *patterns of correlations between observations in a time series*. There are two ways that autocorrelation has been discussed in the literature on the analysis of times series data, including that from single case designs (Huitema & McKean, 1998). In the first, the *correlation between data points separated by specific time lags* is considered. For example, the lag-1 autocorrelation is the correlation between observations one time period apart. This is the correlation between the observations at time t and time $t + 1$ across the length of the time series. Consider the data shown in Figure 1.3, shown again here (Figure 2.1). The data points are, starting at day 1 and going through day 10: 46, 47, 42, 36, 38, 30, 31, 26, 20, and 13.

The lag-1 autocorrelation between these data points is the correlation between the observations at day 1 and day 2; day 2 and day 3; and so forth through days 9 and 10. This autocorrelation is $+0.64$. The lag-2

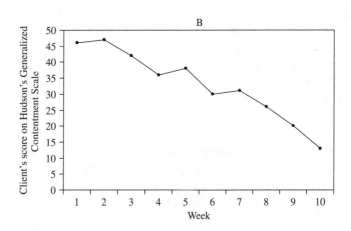

Figure 2.1 Hypothetical B design used to evaluate how a client is doing during the provision of services for depression. [This is Figure 1.3 (from Chapter 1) shown again.]

autocorrelation is the correlation between observations at time t and time $t + 2$, that is, the correlation between observations on day 1 and day 3; day 2 and day 4; and so forth. This lag-2 autocorrelation is $+0.33$. The lag-3 autocorrelation is the correlation between observations at time t and $t + 3$ (in this case, this correlation is $+0.11$); and so forth for any lag k.

The second way in which autocorrelation can be considered is as the correlation between temporally sequential *residuals* from some statistical model fit to a time series. For example, the results of fitting the linear regression model,

$$y_t = B_0 + B_1 t + res_t,$$

to the time series data in Figure 2.1—with y_t the observation at time t, B_0 the model estimated observation at time $t = 0$, B_1 the linear trend of the data across time, and res_t the residual at time t—produces residuals with a lag-1 autocorrelation of -0.204, a lag-2 autocorrelation of -0.017, and a lag-3 autocorrelation of -0.035. The regression model has acted as a *linear filter* (Gottman, 1981) and in a sense removed some of the auto-correlation from the raw data, in this case by explicitly modeling the linear trend in the data (Huitema & McKean, 1998). As emphasized by Huitema and McKean (1998), this leads to an important principle: The residuals from an adequate, well-fitting statistical model applied to a time series will produce residuals that are distributed as *white noise* (see also Ostrom, 1990). White noise residuals are randomly distributed about a mean of zero, with constant variance and *zero autocorrelations at all lags* (Ostrom, 1990). As Huitema and McKean (1998) point out, only under limited circumstances will these two "types" of autocorrelation be the same.

All statistical analysis procedures are based on some set of assumptions. Many statistical procedures potentially used with time series data are based on the assumption that the residuals from the statistical model are *independently distributed*. This implies that the residuals are distributed as white noise; hence, there should be no autocorrelation of any form in the residuals (Ostrom, 1990). If this assumption fails to hold, the consequences for tests of statistical significance can be serious. Positive autocorrelation in the residuals can lead to an underestimate of the standard errors of statistics such as regression coefficients, and to overestimates of test statistics such as t-ratios, resulting in erroneous conclusions based on tests of statistical significance. Ostrom (1990, pp. 21–26) showed how the estimated sampling variance in an estimate of a simple linear regression coefficient can be underestimated by 641%, and the corresponding t-ratio testing the regression coefficient inflated by 395%, when certain patterns of positive autocorrelation are in the time series data. Negative autocorrelation can lead to overestimates of standard errors and underestimates of test statistics. In this case test statistics such as t-ratios are biased downward. The consequences of autocorrelation in residuals from models applied to time series data can be very profound. The reader is strongly urged to read the work of Huitema and McKean (1998), as a good understanding of the issue of autocorrelation will help with subsequent content in this book.

REGRESSION-DISCONTINUITY MODELS

A regression-discontinuity model is one in which there is a break, or discontinuous interruption, in the typical regression model (Neter, Wasserman, & Kutner, 1983). A regression-discontinuity model for a simple AB single case design can be written as,

$$Y_t = B_0 + B_1 t + B_2 X_t + B_3 X_t t + r_t, \tag{2.1}$$

where Y_t is the observation of the dependent variable at time t; t is the time that the observation was made; X_t is a dichotomous *indicator* (Neter et al., 1983) or *dummy* variable (Cohen, Cohen, West, & Aiken, 2003) indicating single case phase (0 = baseline and 1 = treatment); $X_t t$ is the product of the dummy variable X_t and time t; and r_t is the residual from the model for the observation at time t. In this model B_0 is the model estimated value of the dependent variable at time $t = 0$; B_1 is the estimated baseline linear trend; B_2 is the model estimated immediate change in level between baseline and treatment phases, and is the difference between baseline and treatment phase linear trend line intercepts with the time $t = 0$ demarcation line, as shown in Figure 2.2 [this is a third way that "change in level" can be defined (see Chapter 1 for the first two)]; and B_3 is the estimated change in linear trend from baseline to treatment phase.

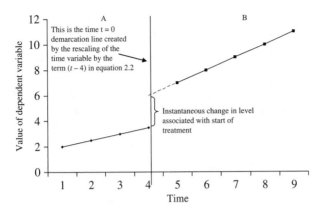

Figure 2.2 An example of a regression-discontinuity model.

Consider the following example of the model expressed by equation 2.1:

$$Y_t = 3.5 + .5(t-4) + 2.5X_t + .5X_t(t-4), \tag{2.2}$$

for $t = 1, 2, \ldots, 9$, where

$X_t = 0$ for $t \leq 4$ (i.e., for baseline phase) and
$X_t = 1$ for $t > 4$ (i.e., for treatment phase),

and where the term $(t-4)$ simply rescales the time variable such that the final baseline point is at time $t = 0$. This regression-discontinuity model is shown in Figure 2.2, and the table of regression coefficients from fitting the regression model 2.2a,

$$Y_t = B_0 + B_1(t-4) + B_2X_t + B_3X_t(t-4) + r_t \tag{2.2a}$$

to the data in Figure 2.2 are shown in Table 2.1. Notice the break between the observations at times $t = 4$ and $t = 5$, where the time series makes a discontinuous, or abrupt, jump (i.e., change) in both level and trend. This sudden change is a *discontinuity* in the otherwise continuous time series. This simple example is of a perfectly fitting regression-discontinuity model. In this model, $B_0 = 3.5$, and is the level of the dependent variable at time $t = 4$, the last baseline point; $B_1 = 0.5$, and represents the

Table 2.1 Regression coefficients from fitting model 2.2a to the data in Figure 2.1 using SPSS version 15

	Unstandardized Coefficients	
Model	B	Std. Error
Constant (intercept)	3.500	0.000
$(t-4)$	0.500	0.000
X_t	2.500	0.000
$X_t(t-4)$	0.500	0.000

baseline linear trend; $B_2 = 2.5$, and is the immediate change in level from baseline to treatment phase and, as shown in Figure 2.2 by the right-facing brace, is the difference between points where the baseline and treatment phase linear trend lines intersect with the vertical line marking the final baseline time point; and $B_3 = 0.5$, and is the change in trend between baseline and treatment phases, so the treatment phase linear trend is $0.5 + 0.5 = 1.0$.

The autocorrelation in the residuals from fitting the regression-discontinuity model (2.1) to an interrupted time series—these residuals form a new time series—would then be modeled using ARIMA methods (Huitema & McKean, 1998; Ostrom, 1990). This analysis approach combining regression and ARIMA techniques has been referred to as a combined *transfer function-disturbance model* (Box, Jenkins, & Reinsel, 1994).

ARIMA MODELS

The term ARIMA is an acronym for *autoregressive integrated moving average*, and ARIMA models are a special class of time series models (Box & Jenkins, 1976; Box, Jenkins, & Reinsel, 2008; McDowell, McCleary, Meidinger, Hay, 1980). The ARIMA models are designated as ARIMA(p,d,q) models, with the p referring to the *autoregressive order* of the model; d indicating the number of times the time series needs to be *differenced* in order to make it stationary (a notion discussed below); and q indicating the *moving average order* of the series. ARIMA models may be applied to interrupted time series designs, such as single case designs, to test intervention effects, as illustrated later (Box & Tiao, 1975).

Stationarity and Order of Differencing

ARIMA models are built upon several assumptions. The first is what is called *stationarity*, an assumption discussed in detail by Cromwell, Labys, and Terraza (1993), who also present a number of tests of this assumption. One way to think of the stationarity assumption is that it states that the characteristics of the time series are invariant across the various epochs—or sections—of the time series. A stationary series will show no temporal trend; hence, applied to a single case design time series, the baseline and treatment phase trends will be zero, and the variance of the series, as well as the autocorrelation structure of the series, across one temporal epoch will be the same across any other temporal epoch. Hence, stationarity is a form of stability.

A time series that shows a temporal trend can be made stationary by *differencing*. In an ARIMA(0,1,0) model, the time series is differenced one lag. This means that the series is transformed by,

$$Y_t - Y_{t-1},$$
$$Y_{t-1} - Y_{t-2},$$
$$Y_{t-2} - Y_{t-3},$$

$$\dots\dots\dots,$$

and so forth.

This first order differencing removes linear trend. In an ARIMA(0,2,0) model, the time series is differenced twice, which involves differencing the first differences defined previously. This second order differencing removes quadratic trend. An ARIMA(0,3,0) model would involve a third-order differencing operation, and so on (McCain & McCleary, 1979; McDowell et al., 1980).

Autoregressive Models

In an autoregressive model, the observations at some previous time lag, or time lags, influence the current observation; there is a relationship between adjacent observations (McClain & McCleary, 1979). An ARIMA(1,0,0) model can be expressed as,

$$Y_t = A_1 Y_{t-1} + s_1, \tag{2.3}$$

where Y_t is the observation at time t; A_1 is a correlation coefficient describing the magnitude of the relationship between the time t and time $t-1$ observations; Y_{t-1} is the time $t-1$ observation; and s_1 is a random *shock* at time t. The term *shock* has also been termed a *disturbance* and is analogous to the residual term in a regression model. The general idea is that at each point in time there may be one or more random factors that affect the observation made at time t. The random shocks are assumed to be normally and independently distributed with mean 0 and constant variance. The term A_1 is limited to the range of values $-1 < A_1 < +1$. This range of values for A_1 serves as the so-called *bounds of stationarity* for the time series. If this condition is not met, the series is *nonstationary*. Conceptually, an ARIMA(1,0,0) model is one in which the preceding temporal observation influences the current observation, and the term A_1 tells by how much (McCain & McCleary, 1979).

An ARIMA(2,0,0) model can be expressed as (McCain & McCleary, 1979),

$$Y_t = A_1 Y_{t-1} + A_2 Y_{t-2} + s_t, \tag{2.4}$$

where the A_1 and A_2 terms are correlation coefficient-like parameters with values between -1 and $+1$, and Y_{t-2} is the time $t-2$ observation. These two terms in the ARIMA(2,0,0) model cannot literally be interpreted as correlation coefficients, though they are similar conceptually. The bounds of stationarity for these terms are given by,

$A_1 + A_2 < 1;$
$A_2 - A_1 < 1;$ and
$|A_2| < 1.$

If these three conditions are not met, then the time series is nonstationary. Conceptually, an ARIMA(2,0,0) model indicates that the two immediately preceding observations influence the current observation, and the terms A_1 and A_2 tell by how much.

There are higher-order ARIMA autoregressive models, such as ARIMA(3,0,0) models, with similar structures, bounds of stationarity, and so forth. The interested reader may consult such sources as Box et al. (2008) for more details.

Moving Average Models

In a moving average model, the *random shock* at some time lag influences the current observation, Y_t; the effects of a random shock endures for a period of time. In an ARIMA(0,0,1) model, the immediately preceding random shock influences the current observation, and this model can be expressed as,

$$Y_t = s_t - M_1 s_{t-1}, \tag{2.5}$$

where M_1 is the first-order moving average term, and s_{t-1} is the random shock at time $t-1$. The term M_1 must lie in the range $-1 < M_1 < 1$ in order for the time series to be stationary. This condition is termed the *bounds of invertibility*. Conceptually, a moving average model says that preceding random shocks influence current observations, and the moving average term tells by how much (McCain & McCleary, 1979).

An ARIMA(0,0,2) model can be expressed as,

$$Y_t = s_t - M_1 s_{t-1} - M_2 s_{t-2}, \tag{2.6}$$

with the bounds of invertibility,

$$M_1 + M_2 < 1;$$
$$M_1 - M_1 < 1; \text{ and}$$
$$|M_2| < 1.$$

If these conditions do not hold, the series is nonstationary. Conceptually, a second-order moving average model says that the two preceding random shocks influence the current observation, Y_t, and the moving average terms tell us by how much (McCain & McCleary, 1979).

Mixed Autoregressive-Moving Average Models

There can also be mixed autoregressive-moving average models. For example, an ARIMA(1,0,1) model can be expressed as (McCain & McCleary, 1979),

$$Y_t = A_1 Y_{t-1} - M_1 s_{t-1} + s_t. \tag{2.7}$$

Conceptually, this model says that the current observation is influenced by the previous observation as well as the previous random shock, and the terms A_1 and M_1 tell by how much.

Autoregressive-Integrated Moving Average Models

The reader should be able to understand now the designation of any ARIMA(p,d,q) model. An ARIMA($1,1,0$) model, for example, is a first-order autoregressive model that required a first differencing operation in order to make the series stationary; an ARIMA($0,2,2$) model is a second-order moving average model that required two differencing operations to make the series stationary; and so forth.

The Complexity of Autocorrelation

One important lesson to take from these various forms of autocorrelation *is the potential complexity of the structure of the relationships between observations in a time series.* Many treatments of autocorrelation in single case design data assume a simple lag-1 autocorrelation. Yet, as the foregoing shows, the autocorrelation in a time series can be much more complex. As noted already at the beginning of the chapter, and as will be seen later, this has implications for the numbers of observations needed to adequately identify the structure of the autocorrelation in a time series.

APPLYING ARIMA MODELS TO TEST INTERVENTIONS

Data sets to which ARIMA methods are applied should have 50 or more data points in the baseline phase (Box & Jenkins, 1976). Before any tests of interventions are carried out, the autocorrelation structure of the time series needs to be modeled. A large number of observations are necessary, as will be seen later, in order to reasonably model the autocorrelation structure of the time series. When an interrupted time series is to be analyzed, the process of modeling the autocorrelation structure of the series focuses on the baseline data since any intervention effect will introduce a form of autocorrelation into the time series, which will eventually be modeled in an analysis of the entire time series (Box et al., 2008; Huitema & McKean, 1998; McCain & McCleary, 1979).

The modeling of the autocorrelation structure is done in a three-phase process: *identification, estimation,* and *diagnosis* (McCain & McCleary, 1979). This three-phase process will be illustrated using interrupted time series data from a study of the effects of implementing a program called aggression replacement training in a runaway shelter (Nugent, Champlin, & Wiinimaki, 1997).

Testing Assumptions

The first step is to test the assumptions of stationarity, constant variance, and normality associated with ARIMA models. Cromwell et al. (1993) describe a number of tests for these assumptions. These assumptions need to be tested, especially stationarity, before moving on to the next steps. In the interest of the brevity of this book, only one of these tests will be described here. The reader is referred to Cromwell et al. (1993) for in-depth discussion of the full range of tests.

The one test for stationarity that will be outlined and illustrated is the so-called *Dickey-Fuller test for a unit root* (Cromwell et al., 1993; Dickey & Fuller, 1979). This would be conducted on the baseline data as follows:

(1) Form the first difference variable, $\Delta y_t = y_t - y_{t-1}$.

(2) Fit the regression model, $\Delta y_t = \delta y_{t-1} + r_t$. In this regression model without a constant, the term δ is the regression coefficient for the regression of the observation of the dependent variable (i.e., $\Delta y_t = y_t - y_{t-1}$) at time t on the observation at time $t-1$, y_{t-1}. This is a test for a so-called *unit root*.

(3) Fit the regression model, $\Delta y_t = B_0 + \delta y_{t-1} + r_t$. This is the same regression model as in (2) but with the intercept term, B_0. This is a test for a *unit root with drift*.

(4) Fit the regression model, $\Delta y_t = B_0 + B_1 t + \delta y_{t-1} + r_t$. This is the regression model in (3) but with the trend term, B_1, added, and is a test for a *unit root with drift relative to a stochastic trend*.

(5) Compare the t-ratios for the δ term against tabled values that can be found in Cromwell et al. (1993) and Dickey and Fuller (1979). *If the results of the test of statistical significance of the δ term in these statistical models are statistically significant, the time series tested is deemed to be stationary.*

The rationale for this test is discussed in Cromwell et al. (1993) and the reader is referred to this source for details. Also included in Cromwell et al.'s discussion are details on the concept of the unit root and its importance. In the interest of brevity, this concept is not discussed further here.

Identification

In the identification phase, plots of the *autocorrelation* and *partial autocorrelation functions* are inspected. The autocorrelation function relates the values of the time series at one point in time with the values at some time lag in the past. As discussed earlier, the lag-1 autocorrelation is the correlation between the series value, y_t, and that at the immediately preceding point in time, y_{t-1}; the lag-2 autocorrelation is the correlation between the series values y_t and y_{t-2}; and so forth. The autocorrelation function is computed and graphically plotted for lags covering about 25% of the total duration of the baseline series (McCain & McCleary, 1979). The pattern of autocorrelations in this plot is then inspected for evidence of an autoregressive process, a moving average process, or both, as detailed later.

The partial autocorrelation function relates the values of the series at a time t with those at a time lag $t-q$, controlling for the correlations between time series observations at lags between t and $t-q$. The patterns in the partial autocorrelation function for the time series are also diagnostic for the type of ARIMA model that best represents the autocorrelation structure of the time series (McCain & McCleary, 1979).

Identification of Autoregressive Processes.   In an autoregressive model of order p, symbolized by AR(p), the autocorrelation function (ACF) will show an exponentially decaying, sinusoidally decaying, or combination of an exponentially and sinusoidally decaying pattern of autocorrelations, as illustrated in Figure 2.3 for an AR process of order one [i.e., an AR(1) process]. Notice in this figure that the magnitudes of the autocorrelations decrease across lags in an oscillating manner, with the maximum magnitude at later lags lower than that at the earliest lags. This is an example of a combined exponentially-sinusoidally decaying autocorrelation pattern suggestive of an AR process (Box & Jenkins, 1976; McCain & McCleary, 1979).

The partial autocorrelation function (PACF) for an AR process of order p will show p significant spikes at the first p lags, and then a sharp

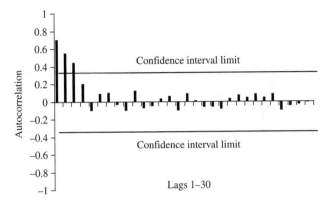

Figure 2.3 Autocorrelation function (ACF) of an ARIMA(1,0,0) process where A_1 is positive.

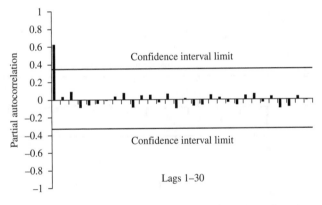

Figure 2.4 Partial autocorrelation function (PACF) of an ARIMA(1,0,0) process where A_1 is positive.

cutoff to a white noise (i.e., random) process across the remaining lags. For example, Figure 2.4 shows an example of a PACF for an AR(1) process with A_1 positive. Notice the significant positive lag-1 autocorrelation, followed by an abrupt cutoff to randomly dispersed, statistically nonsignificant partial autocorrelations, the signature of white noise.

Figures 2.5 and 2.6 show illustrative ACFs and PACFs suggestive of an AR(1) process in which the autoregressive parameter A_1 is negative. Notice how the ACF rapidly oscillates from positive to negative in an

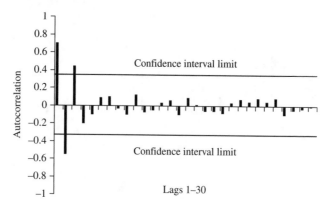

Figure 2.5 Autocorrelation function (ACF) of an ARIMA(1,0,0) process where A_1 is negative.

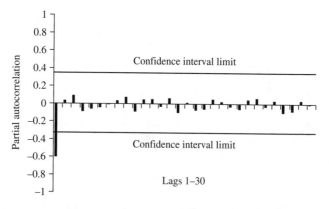

Figure 2.6 Partial autocorrelation function (PACF) of an ARIMA(1,0,0) process where A_1 is negative.

exponentially decaying manner. Note further how the PACF shows a single significant partial autocorrelation at lag 1 that is negative, followed by a pattern consistent with white noise.

Figures 2.7 and 2.8 show an illustrative ACF and a PACF for an AR(2) process with both A_1 and A_2 positive. Note in particular the manner in which the PACF shows two significant spikes at lags 1 and 2, and then cuts off to a pattern consistent with white noise.

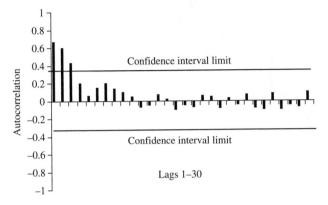

Figure 2.7 Autocorrelation function (ACF) of an ARIMA(2,0,0) process where both A_1 and A_2 are positive.

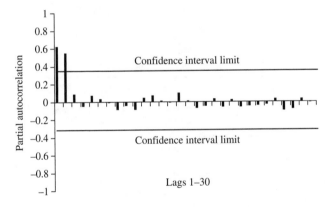

Figure 2.8 Partial autocorrelation function (PACF) of an ARIMA(2,0,0) process where both A_1 and A_2 are positive.

Identification of Moving Average Processes.   The ACF and PACF patterns for moving average (MA) processes are the *opposite of those for autoregressive processes*. For example, consider Figures 2.9 and 2.10. These show illustrative ACF and PACF functions for a moving average process of order one [i.e., an MA(1) process] with the M_1 parameter positive. Note in the ACF the single significant spike at lag 1, followed by a pattern consistent with white noise. Note how this is the opposite of an AR process; if this pattern were to appear in the PACF as opposed to the

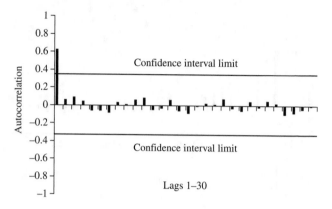

Figure 2.9 Autocorrelation function (ACF) of an ARIMA(0,0,1) process where M_1 is positive.

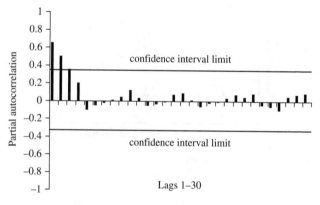

Figure 2.10 Partial autocorrelation function (PACF) of an ARIMA(0,0,1) process where M_1 is positive.

ACF it would be consistent with an AR(1) process. The PACF in Figure 2.10 shows an exponentially decaying sinusoidal pattern. If appearing in the ACF, this pattern would be consistent with an AR(1) process.

Figures 2.11 and 2.12 show an ACF and a PACF consistent with an MA(2) process with M_1 positive and M_2 negative. Note in the ACF the two significant spikes at lags 1 and 2, with the lag-1 spike positive and the lag-2 spike negative, followed by a pattern suggestive of white noise. This pattern, if seen in the PACF, would be suggestive of an AR(2) process

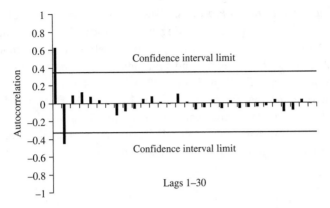

Figure 2.11 Autocorrelation function (ACF) of an ARIMA(0,0,2) process where M_1 is positive and M_2 is negative.

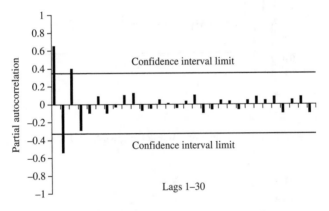

Figure 2.12 Partial autocorrelation function (PACF) of an ARIMA(0,0,2) process where M_1 is positive and M_2 is negative.

with the A_1 parameter positive and the A_2 parameter negative. Note in the PACF the rapidly oscillating positive and negative spikes that are decaying in an exponential manner. This pattern is consistent with an MA(2) process with the M_1 parameter positive and the M_2 parameter negative. As discussed previously, if this pattern were observed in the ACF, it would be suggestive of an AR(2) process with the A_1 parameter positive and the A_2 parameter negative.

Identification of Mixed Processes.   The patterns in both the ACF and PACF for an autoregressive-moving average process (ARMA) of order p,q, ARMA(p,q) [i.e., an ARIMA($p,0,q$) model] will show complex combinations of exponential and sinusoidal decay. For example, consider the ACF and PACF in Figures 2.13 and 2.14. The patterns in mixed models are such that there is no clear way, as in the AR(p) (for which the PACF can be used to estimate order) and MA(q) (for which the ACF can be used to estimate order) models, to determine the order of the autoregressive and/or moving average processes. In this case, a

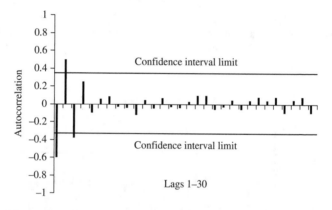

Figure 2.13 Autocorrelation function (ACF) of an ARIMA(1,0,1) process.

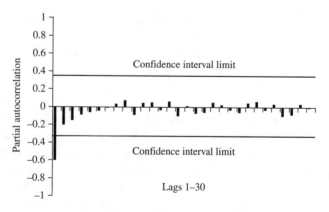

Figure 2.14 Partial autocorrelation function (PACF) of an ARIMA(1,0,1) process.

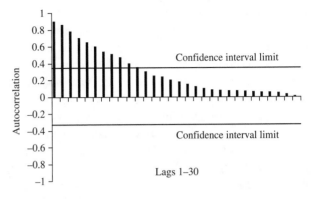

Figure 2.15 Autocorrelation function (ACF) of a nonstationary time series.

trial-and-error method will need to be followed to identify the autoregressive-moving average process.

Identification of Differencing Order.   The ACF and PACF can also be used to identify a series that is not stationary. Consider the ACF in Figure 2.15. Note the slowly decaying pattern of significant autocorrelations. This pattern is consistent with a time series with a gradually increasing trend across time and suggests the need for a first-order differencing in order to make the series stationary. This pattern would imply that the analyst needs to consider a model of the form ARIMA(p,1,q).

Statistical Tests for Autocorrelation.   Numerous statistical tests have been developed to test for statistically significant autocorrelations in time series data (see, e.g., Cromwell et al., 1993). Only one will be mentioned here, and illustrated later, the so-called Box-Ljung statistic [also called the Ljung-Box, or Q-, statistic (Cromwell et al., 1993; McCain & McCleary, 1979)]. This chi-square statistic, with k degrees of freedom, can be used to test the null hypothesis, loosely stated, that the autocorrelations across k time lags are patterned as white noise. A statistically significant outcome would imply that some form of autocorrelation pattern exists in the time series.

Another form of test is that of individual autocorrelations in an ACF. This is typically done by viewing the ACF and determining whether an autocorrelation is of sufficient magnitude to exceed the confidence interval bounds plotted on the ACF, as can be seen in earlier and subsequent figures (McCain & McCleary, 1979). These bounds are approximate 95% confidence interval bounds, and any autocorrelation that exceeds these can be considered to be statistically significant. However, in any ACF plot there can be one to two individual autocorrelations that exceed these bounds in every 30 lags just by chance. The use of the Box-Ljung (or comparable) statistic can be used to conduct a statistical test over a *set* of autocorrelations. For example, if the ACF has been plotted to 30 lags, the Box-Ljung statistic with 30 degrees of freedom would test the null hypothesis, again loosely stated, that the 30 autocorrelations are patterned as white noise. Ideally, the analyst will make use of both formal statistical tests and visual inspections of ACF and PACF plots when working to identify an autocorrelation process.

Summary of Identification.   The first step in the analysis of a time series using ARIMA methods is to inspect ACF and PACF plots, and to use formal tests of statistical significance, to assess the assumption of stationarity and to form hypotheses as to the existence and form of autocorrelation in the series. The stationarity of the series is assessed using ACF plots as well as tests for stationarity, such as the Dickey-Fuller test, described by Cromwell et al. (1993). Once the series has been deemed stationary, or differenced sufficiently to make it stationary, the analyst inspects ACF and PACF plots that can be produced by any of a wide range of computer packages, such as those shown later that came from the use of SPSS version 15. The analyst looks for the patterns consistent with those described previously and frames a tentative hypothesis as to the form of the autocorrelation process in the series, such as an ARIMA(1,0,0) model. This model is then estimated in the second step, that of *estimation*.

Model Estimation and Model Diagnosis

Once a tentative ARIMA model has been identified, the parameters of the model are estimated, using a program such as the time series option in SPSS version 15. The residuals from this estimated model are computed, and then tested for the presence of autocorrelation processes using the methods described previously in the identification process. If the presence of significant residual autocorrelation is identified, the model is respecified and then the residuals checked for the presence of autocorrelation processes. This iterative process continues until there is no residual autocorrelation in the residuals from the model representing the autocorrelation in the time series. This ARIMA model is then used to represent the autocorrelation structure of the time series, with subsequent models fit to the entire interrupted time series in an effort to test intervention effects. This process will now be illustrated using data from an evaluation of the implementation of an aggression replacement training program in a runaway shelter (Nugent et al., 1997).

ILLUSTRATIVE DATA ANALYSIS

The ARIMA procedures will now be illustrated by analyzing an interrupted time series that came from a study of the implementation of an aggression replacement training program for adolescents in a runaway shelter (Nugent et al., 1997). The design of this program evaluation was essentially an AB single system design, with the system studied being the adolescents residing in the shelter. The baseline phase was composed of 309 daily observations of antisocial behavior engaged in by residents, while the treatment phase consisted of 210 daily observations of the adolescents' antisocial behavior that occurred while aggression replacement training was provided for each resident in the shelter. The daily numbers of adolescents, male and female, residing in the shelter were recorded as well. The dependent variable in the illustrative analysis that follows was the *daily rate of antisocial behavior*, obtained by dividing the total number of antisocial behaviors recorded for a particular day by the total number of residents in the shelter that day. The daily rate of antisocial behavior, shown as an AB single case design graphic, is shown in Figure 2.16.

Tests of Assumptions

The results of a Dickey-Fuller test for the presence of a unit root were statistically significant [$\hat{\delta} = -0.22$, $t(307) = -6.1$, $p < 0.01$], as were those for the presence of a unit root plus random drift [$\hat{\delta} = -0.72$,

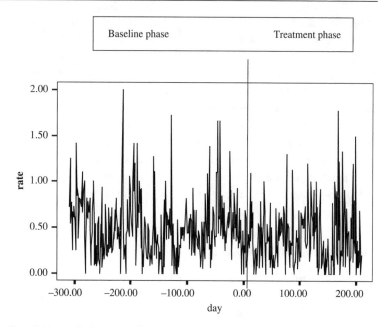

Figure 2.16 AB single system design daily rate of antisocial behavior data from evaluation of aggression replacement training program by Nugent, Champlin, and Wiinimaki (1997).

$t(306) = -13.2$, $p < 0.01$] and the results for a model with unit root plus random drift relative to a stochastic trend [$\hat{\delta} = -0.73$, $t(305) = -13.2$, $p < 0.01$]. All of these results were consistent with the baseline series being stationary. The 310 baseline observations were split into three sections and F-tests for homogeneity of variance conducted, with all results consistent with homogeneity of variance across the baseline series. Assessments of normality suggested no serious departures from this assumption.

Identification

As noted earlier, when analyzing time series data with a baseline/treatment, or preintervention/postintervention, structure, the ACF and PACF of the baseline (or preintervention) series should be studied through lags covering about 25% of the length of the series for purposes of identifying the autocorrelation patterns. The goal of this part of the analysis is to model the "steady state" of the baseline time series so that changes to this steady state concomitant with, and subsequent to, the start of the intervention can be identified.

The ACF and PACF for the baseline data, estimated using SPSS version 15, on the daily rate of antisocial behavior from the runaway shelter study are shown through 60 lags in Figures 2.17 and 2.18. The Box-Ljung statistic for these autocorrelations across 60 lags was $\chi^2(60) = 138.4$, $p < 0.001$, results suggestive of significant autocorrelation in the baseline time series. The pattern of autocorrelations in the ACF shows a decaying sinusoidal pattern. The PACF shows two significant spikes at lags 1 and 2, both positive, with a cutoff after lag 2. These patterns are suggestive of a second-order autoregressive process with both A_1 and A_2 positive.

Estimation

The results of fitting an ARIMA(2,0,0) model, using SPSS version 15, to the baseline time series are shown in Table 2.2. As can be seen in this table, both first- and second-order autoregressive parameters were

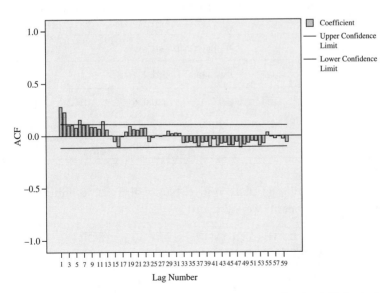

Figure 2.17 Autocorrelation function (ACF) for "daily rate of antisocial behavior" baseline data.

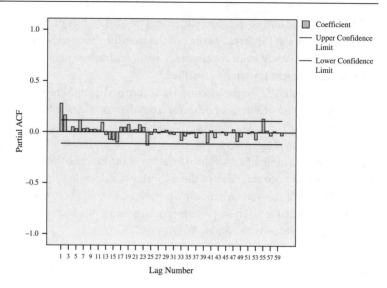

Figure 2.18 Partial autocorrelation function (PACF) for "daily rate of antisocial behavior" baseline data.

Table 2.2 Results of fitting ARIMA(2,0,0) model to baseline time series using SPSS version 15

		Parameter Estimates			
		Estimates	Std. Error	t	p
Autoregressive parameters	AR(1)	0.231	0.056	4.100	<0.001
	AR(2)	0.165	0.056	2.935	0.004
Constant		0.508	0.030	17.146	<0.001

statistically significant and positive. Notice that the conditions for bounds of stationarity were also met:

$$A_1 + A_2 = 0.231 + 0.165 < 1;$$
$$A_2 - A_1 = 0.165 - 0.231 < 1; \text{ and}$$
$$|A_2| = |0.165| < 1.$$

The constant in this model, 0.508, gives the mean daily rate of antisocial behavior in the shelter during baseline phase.

Diagnosis or Model Checking

The ACF and PACF through 60 lags for the residuals from fitting this ARIMA(2,0,0) model to the baseline time series are shown in Figures 2.19 and 2.20. The Box-Ljung statistic for these autocorrelations was $\chi^2(60) = 46.6$, $p > 0.80$, a result consistent with the residual autocorrelations being white noise. The patterns in the ACF and PACF were also consistent with the residual autocorrelations being a white noise process. These results suggested that the ARIMA(2,0,0) model adequately represented the autocorrelation structure in the baseline data.

Test of Effect of Aggression Replacement Training

Now that a model of the baseline steady state has been developed and checked for adequacy, the possible impact that the implementation of the aggression replacement training (ART) program may have had on

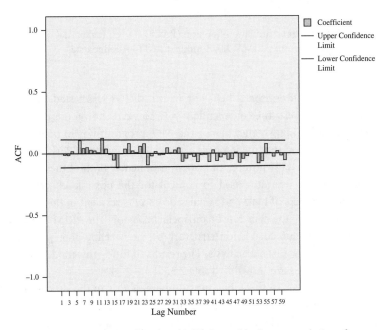

Figure 2.19 Autocorrelation function (ACF) for residual autocorrelations from ARIMA(2,0,0) model fitted to baseline data.

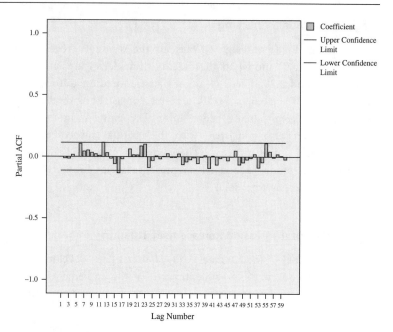

Figure 2.20 Partial autocorrelation function (PACF) for residual partial autocorrelations from ARIMA(2,0,0) model fitted to baseline data.

the daily rate of antisocial behavior in the shelter was tested. In this analysis, there were three independent variables: a dichotomous dummy variable indicating whether or not the ART program was in operation (0 = baseline; 1 = treatment phase); the daily number of girls in the shelter; and the daily number of boys in the shelter. Both of these latter variables were covariates used to control for the possible effects that differing numbers of male and female adolescents resident in the shelter may have had on the daily rate of antisocial behavior. The ARIMA(2,0,0) model for the autocorrelation structure of the baseline data was also included in the statistical analysis. The results of fitting this model to the entire time series are shown in Table 2.3.

As can be seen in this table, the numbers of girls in the shelter on a given day was associated with the daily rate of antisocial behavior, $b = -0.023$, $t = -2.24$, $p < 0.05$, with the negative parameter indicating that, holding number of boys constant, as the number of girls in the shelter increased, the daily rate of antisocial behavior decreased. The

Table 2.3 Results of fitting ARIMA(2,0,0) model to entire time series testing effect of implementation of aggression replacement training program

		Estimates	Std. Error	t	p
Autoregressive parameters	AR(1)	0.178	0.044	4.052	< 0.001
	AR(2)	0.111	0.044	2.518	0.012
Regression coefficients	Number of boys in shelter	−0.002	0.011	−0.144	0.886
	Number of girls in shelter	−0.023	0.010	−2.238	0.026
	Aggression replacement training (0 = baseline; 1 = ART)	−0.113	0.040	−2.802	0.005
Constant		0.654	0.111	5.866	< 0.001

ART, aggression replacement training.

parameter estimate for the ART program was also statistically significant, $b = -0.113$, $t = -2.8$, $p < 0.05$. The negative sign on this parameter indicated that, controlling for numbers of boys and girls in the shelter each day, the ART program was associated with a decrease in the daily rate of antisocial behavior in the shelter.

The Box-Ljung statistic for the residual autocorrelations from this model was $\chi^2(60) = 64.51$, $p > 0.30$, results consistent with the residual autocorrelations being white noise. The ACF and PACF for these residual autocorrelations can be seen in Figures 2.21 and 2.22. In both cases, the patterns in the ACF and PACF were consistent with white noise processes. These results imply that the model developed adequately represented the autocorrelation structure in the time series.

Alternate Models of Intervention Effects

There are ARIMA models that can be used to represent different forms of intervention effects. The aforementioned ARIMA model compares phase means, and can also be interpreted as indicating an immediate change in mean level in the dependent variable since both baseline and treatment

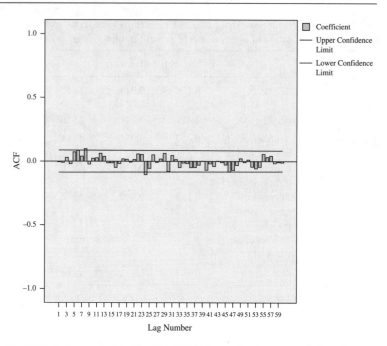

Figure 2.21 Autocorrelation function (ACF) for residual autocorrelations from fitting ARIMA(2,0,0) model to entire time series in which effects of aggression replacement training was tested.

phase time series appear to be stationary relative to the phase means. This form of immediate change in level can be conceived of as a *step function* form of a *transfer function* (McCain & McCleary, 1979). A step function form of transfer function is shown in Figure 2.23. A transfer function describes the effect that an intervention has on a dependent variable. The step function shown in Figure 2.23 shows that the intervention appears to have an immediate effect on the dependent variable, decreasing the level from the stable baseline level to a new stable treatment phase level. The transfer function in Figure 2.24, in comparison, shows an intervention effect that is more gradual, with the final effect an asymptotic new constant level. The transfer function illustrated in Figure 2.24 can be tested by fitting the statistical model (McCain & McCleary, 1979),

$$y_t = B_0 + B_1 y_{t-1} X_t + B_2 X_t + r_t, \tag{2.8}$$

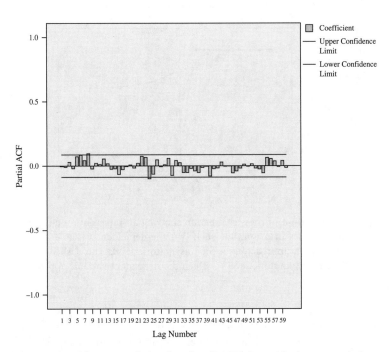

Figure 2.22 Partial autocorrelation function (PACF) for residual autocorrelations from fitting ARIMA(2,0,0) model to entire time series in which effects of aggression replacement training was tested.

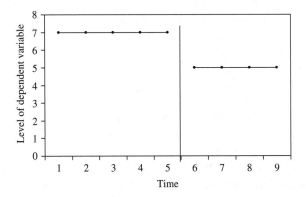

Figure 2.23 A step function form of transfer function.

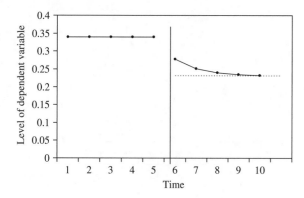

Figure 2.24 Illustration of transfer function showing an intervention effect that gradually increases in magnitude such that the dependent variable slowly decreases in level, approaching a final asymptotic level. The dashed line shows the final asymptotic level to which the dependent variable approaches in time.

to the interrupted time series, where B_0 is the baseline mean level of the dependent variable; B_1 is a parameter describing the gradually decelerating impact of the intervention on the dependent variable; B_2 is the immediate change in level associated with the start of the intervention; and X_t is the dummy variable such that $X_t = 0$ for baseline and $X_t = 1$ for treatment. The appearance of the term y_{t-1} on the right side of equation 2.8 makes this model one with a lagged value of the dependent variable (Ostrom, 1990). The asymptotic (i.e., final) value of the change in level of the dependent variable associated with implementation of the intervention is given by,

$$\frac{B_2}{1 - B_1},\tag{2.9}$$

where B_1 and B_2 are the values of the corresponding parameters in model 2.8 (McCain & McCleary, 1979).

The results of fitting model 2.8 to the interrupted time series data from the Nugent et al. (1997) study were statistically nonsignificant for the gradual form of the intervention effect shown in Figure 2.24. The intervention effect in the case of the Nugent et al. (1997) study appears to be more immediate than gradual. This is also implied by the estimated value of the B_1 term from model 2.8 when the model was fit to the Nugent et al. (1997) data. This estimated value was –0.14. This small value implies a more immediate intervention effect (McCain & McCleary, 1979).

There are a variety of other transfer function forms that describe various forms of intervention effects. The interested reader is referred to Box and Tiao (1975) for further details.

MORE ON REGRESSION-DISCONTINUITY MODELS

The use of regression-discontinuity models with single case design data would involve:

(a) Fitting a regression model, such as that in equation 2.1, to the interrupted time series from a single case design and saving the unstandardized residuals

(b) Computing the autocorrelation and partial autocorrelation functions for the unstandardized residuals

(c) Identifying the autocorrelation structure (autoregressive; moving average; mixed) of the residuals using the procedures discussed above

(d) Refitting the model but including the autocorrelation structure identified in (c), and saving the residuals from this model

(e) Investigating the autocorrelation and partial autocorrelation functions for these new residuals. If autocorrelation is still present, return to step (c) and reidentify the autocorrelation structure. If no autocorrelation is present, then estimate the entire model and interpret the results of the analysis (Huitema & McKean, 1998; Ostrom, 1990).

Box, Jenkins, and Reinsel (2008) referred to this approach as a combined *transfer function-disturbance model*. The specific form of equation 2.1 that would be used would be informed by a visual analysis of the single case design data. For example, if there is an apparent baseline trend, an apparent immediate change in level, and an apparent change in trend across the A/B phase transition, then the full model expressed as equation 2.1 could be tested for adequacy.

However, if, say, there is no apparent change in level across the A/B phase transition, while there is an apparent change in trend, then the B_2 term could be set to zero in 2.1, giving the regression model,

$$y_t = B_0 + B_1 t + B_3 X_t t + r_t, \tag{2.10}$$

which is a special case of 2.1. This model explicitly represents baseline linear trend; final baseline level of the dependent variable; and change in linear trend across the A/B phase transition. Similarly, if there is no apparent baseline trend and no change in trend, but a possible change in level across the A/B phase transition, then the parameters B_1 and B_3 can be set to zero and the model,

$$y_t = B_0 + B_2 X_t + r_t \tag{2.11}$$

fit to the data from the single case design. This model explicitly represents baseline mean level, and change in mean level, across the A/B phase transition. As noted previously, the residuals from fitting the appropriate regression-discontinuity model would be tested for autocorrelation using ARIMA methods.

Illustrative Analysis One

The aforementioned approach to using regression-discontinuity models could be used with the data from the Nugent et al. (1997) study. In this case, a visual analysis of the data in Figure 2.16 suggests neither a baseline trend nor any apparent change in trend across the A/B phase transition. Statistical analyses of baseline trend ($b = -0.0003$, $t = -0.85$, $p > 0.30$) and treatment phase trend ($b = 0.0004$, $t = 0.37$, $p > 0.70$) corroborate these visual impressions. The details of these statistical analyses are omitted in the interest of space.

Thus, the model in equation 2.11 is fit to the data and the unstandardized residuals saved. Inspections of the autocorrelation and partial autocorrelation functions for these residuals, omitted here in the interest of space, suggest a second-order autoregressive process. The estimation of the two autoregressive parameters reveals both to be statistically significant, and inspections of the autocorrelation and partial autocorrelation functions from this model of the residuals show no evidence of residual autocorrelation. Adding the second-order autoregressive model for the residuals to the model in equation 2.11 leads to the same results, shown previously for the ARIMA(2,0,0) analysis, concerning the effects of implementing ART in the runaway shelter.

A Second Illustrative Analysis

The regression-discontinuity analysis procedure will be further illustrated by analyzing the data from the A and B_1 phases of the single case design in Figure 1.2. This analysis of data from an actual single case design will illustrate several important issues concerning the use of such models with short time series. Figure 1.2 is shown again as Figure 2.25, with baseline linear trend (solid line), treatment linear trend (dashed line), and immediate change in level—as represented by difference between the intercepts of the baseline and treatment phase linear trend lines at the A/B phase transition—shown in the graph. These graphic aids all suggest a linear baseline trend, an immediate change in level across the A/B phase transition, and a change in linear trend from baseline to treatment phase. Hence, the model in equation 2.1 was fit to the data, and Table 2.4 shows these results, with the time variable scaled such that the last baseline

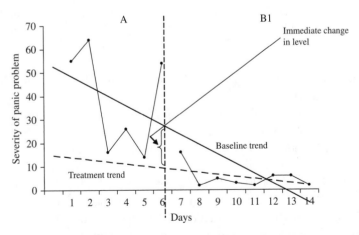

Figure 2.25 Reproduction of first two phases from Figure 1.4 from Chapter 1, with baseline linear trend (*solid line*), treatment linear trend (*dashed line*), and immediate change in level represented.

Table 2.4 Regression coefficients from fitting regression-discontinuity model (2.1) to the data in Figure 2.24

Model	Unstandardized Coefficients		Standardized Coefficients		
	B	Std. Error	Beta	t	p
1 (Constant)	27.810	10.841		2.565	0.028
t	−4.143	3.581	−0.788	−1.157	0.274
x	−18.488	15.929	−0.432	−1.161	0.273
xt	3.238	4.262	0.431	0.760	0.465

t = time of observation; x = dummy variable indicating phase (0 = baseline, 1 = treatment), and xt = product of t and x.

Table 2.5 Autocorrelations through lag 5 for residuals from fitting regression-discontinuity model (2.1) to data from Figure 2.24

Lag	Autocorrelation		Box-Ljung Statistic		
	Value of autocorrelation	Std. error	Value of Box-Ljung statistic	df	p
1	−0.096	0.241	0.158	1	0.691
2	−0.210	0.231	0.984	2	0.611
3	−0.485	0.222	5.777	3	0.123
4	0.085	0.211	5.937	4	0.204
5	0.197	0.200	6.908	5	0.228

measure is at time $t = 0$. The appropriateness of this analysis will be considered later.

Table 2.5 shows the autocorrelations through lag 5 for the residuals from this model, while Figure 2.26 shows these autocorrelations graphically. Figure 2.27 shows the PACF for these residuals. *Notice that any patterns in these autocorrelations and partial autocorrelations are much more difficult to distinguish because of the small number of data points.* The lag-3 autocorrelation and the lag-3 partial autocorrelation in these figures are statistically significant, which might – cautiously – be interpreted as suggesting a statistically significant third-order autoregressive parameter.

Table 2.6 shows the results of fitting an ARIMA(3,0,0) model to these residuals from the regression-discontinuity model, thereby simultaneously

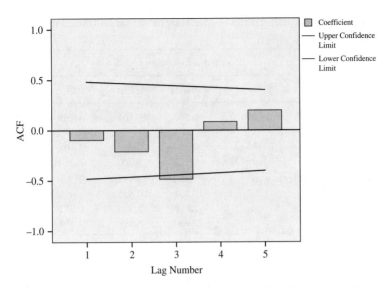

Figure 2.26 Autocorrelations through lag 5 for residuals from fitting regression-discontinuity model (2.1) to data from Figure 2.24.

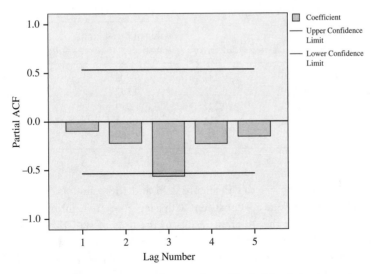

Figure 2.27 Partial autocorrelation function for residuals from fitting regression-discontinuity model (2.1) to data from Figure 2.24.

Table 2.6 Results from regression-discontinuity model with ARIMA(3,0,0) model for residuals

Parameter Estimates					
		Estimates	Std. Error	t	p
Autoregressive parameters	AR(1)	−0.330	0.264	−1.249	0.252
	AR(2)	−0.390	0.232	−1.682	0.137
	AR(3)	−0.728	0.200	−3.639	0.008
Regression coefficients	t	−3.250	2.499	−1.301	0.235
	x	−15.851	10.595	−1.496	0.089*
	xt	1.858	2.406	0.772	0.465
Constant		27.460	6.389	4.298	0.004

* One-tailed test.

Table 2.7 Autocorrelations through lag 5 for residuals from model (2.1) fitted to data from Figure 2.24 with ARIMA(3,0,0) autocorrelation structure in residuals

			Box-Ljung Statistic		
Lag	Value of auto-correlation	Std. Error	Value of Box-Ljung statistic	df	p
1	−0.216	0.241	0.803	1	0.370
2	−0.059	0.231	0.867	2	0.648
3	−0.086	0.222	1.019	3	0.797
4	−0.193	0.211	1.854	4	0.763
5	0.147	0.200	2.389	5	0.793

modeling the time series in Figure 2.25 and the residuals from this model. These results are consistent with a lag-3 negative autoregressive parameter. Note the different results of the tests of statistical significance for the parameters in Table 2.5, where the autocorrelation in the residuals is not modeled, and those in Table 2.6, where it is modeled as an ARIMA(3,0,0) process. The results in Table 2.6 suggest the possibility of a statistically significant immediate decrease in level across the A/B phase change.

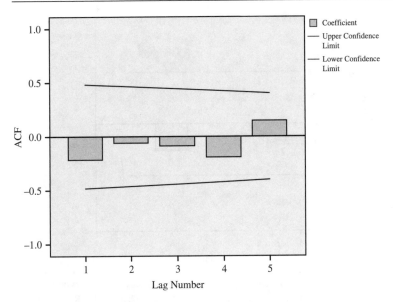

Figure 2.28 Autocorrelation function for residuals from regression-discontinuity model (2.1) fitted to data from Figure 2.24, with ARIMA(3,0,0) model for autocorrelation in residuals.

The autocorrelations in the residuals from the model in Table 2.6 are shown in Table 2.7 and in Figure 2.28. There is now little evidence of any autocorrelation in the residuals. The partial autocorrelation function is shown in Figure 2.29.

The problem with this analysis is, of course, that it is based on a very, very small number of data points. Specifying a lag-3 autoregressive structure in the residuals based on this very small number of data points is (1) an endeavor fraught with enormous risk of error and (2) downright foolish. This highlights one of the criticisms levied against the use of statistical procedures, such as the regression-discontinuity models, with the small numbers of observations typically found in single case design studies—*the application of complex statistical inference methods with very small numbers of observations.* This issue is considered later in further detail.

One option in a case such as this would be the explicit testing of alternate models that appear to be plausible. Different autocorrelation structures could also be fit to the residuals from the regression-discontinuity

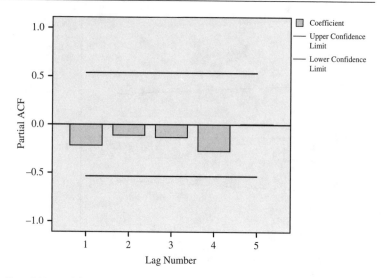

Figure 2.29 Partial autocorrelation function for residuals from regression-discontinuity model (2.1) fitted to data from Figure 2.24, with ARIMA(3,0,0) model for autocorrelation in residuals.

model, and then the differences in results across the different models compared. This would be a form of sensitivity analysis, in this case a test of the extent to which the results of the test of intervention effects are sensitive to the autocorrelation structure imposed upon the residuals.

The analyst could also fit different forms of regression-discontinuity models to the AB data. This would allow the explicit testing of alternate ways of modeling the across-phase changes. For example, in lieu of the model in equation 2.1, the analyst could fit a form of the model in equation 2.11,

$$y_t = B_0 + B_1 X_t + r_t,$$

where B_0 is the baseline mean level of the dependent variable, X_t is the dummy variable such that $X = 0$ for baseline and $X = 1$ for treatment phase, and B_1 is the change in mean level across the phase change. This model assumes that the baseline trend is zero, and that the change in trend across the A/B phase change is zero, and therefore is a special case of the model in equation 2.1.

Table 2.8 Results of fitting model in equation 2.11 to data from Figure 2.24 using ordinary least squares regression methods

		Coefficients				
		Unstandardized Coefficients		Standardized Coefficients		
Model		B	Std. Error	Beta	t	p
1	(Constant)	35.000	5.843		5.990	<0.001
	X	-31.286	8.263	-0.738	-3.786	0.003

The autocorrelation and partial autocorrelation functions for the residuals from fitting this regression model to the data from Figure 2.25 show no evidence of significant autocorrelations or partial autocorrelations. The ordinary least squares (OLS) results from this model, shown in Table 2.8, may therefore be used and interpreted (Huitema & McKean, 1998). The lag-3 autoregressive model tentatively identified for the residuals from the regression-discontinuity model 2.1 fit to these data can therefore be hypothesized to be a consequence of misspecification of the regression model (Huitema & McKean, 1998). These conclusions, however, must be tempered by the realization that the time series is short, and so the assessment of autocorrelation is based on low-power tests.

If the results of these different approaches converge on a common outcome, then the analyst can be more confident that the results are not overly sensitive to the analytic approach taken. Conversely, if the results vary considerably across the different analytic approaches, then the analyst must recognize that the outcome of the analysis is dependent upon how the data are analyzed. In the case of the data in Figure 2.25, the results of both analyses converge to suggest a significant change in level across the A/B_1 phase transition. From a statistical perspective, even this conclusion must be viewed from the perspective of the very clear indication that the variance of the residuals about the baseline mean line and that about the treatment phase mean line are very likely heterogeneous, a violation of the homogeneity of variance assumption used in OLS regression methods (Neter et al. 1983).

GENERAL ISSUES IN THE ANALYSIS OF SINGLE CASE DESIGN DATA

The analysis methods discussed previously point to a number of issues that are of importance in all analyses of single case design data. These issues should be kept in mind by the reader as he or she reads the following chapters. The principle issue concerns the length of the time series. This issue has already been discussed at the end of Chapter 1. Figure 1.17 from Chapter 1 is shown again here as Figure 2.30.

It was shown in Chapter 1, using Figure 2.30, how a short time series may invite the analyst to see, by way of the overinterpretation of random variation, patterns that do not exist. The longer the time series, the less likely the analyst will misinterpret random variation as systematic variation. This is illustrated by the short time series between the vertical lines in Figure 2.30, and shown separately in Figure 2.31. The data in Figure 2.31, if it were a four-data point baseline, could readily be interpreted as showing an increasing trend. The longer time series in Figure 2.30, however, if it were a 30-data point baseline, would make it easier for the analyst to assess the variation in the time series for randomness and systematic trend.

A related issue concerns the identification of patterns of autocorrelation. While some have argued that autocorrelation is not as prevalent in single case design data as many fear (e.g., Huitima, 1985, 1986; see Busk & Marascuilo, 1988, for counterargument), the potential problems in statistical analyses caused by autocorrelated residuals can be serious and

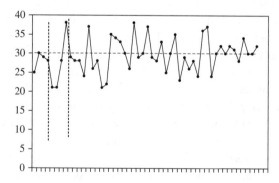

Figure 2.30 This is Figure 1.17 from Chapter 1 showing a 30-data point time series composed of random variation about a constant mean of 30.

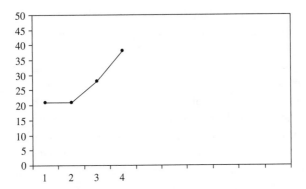

Figure 2.31 Possible four-data point baseline phase abstracted from 30-data point time series in Figure 2.29. These are the four data points shown between the two vertical lines in Figure 2.29.

hence should be neither underestimated nor ignored (Ostrom, 1990). Further, as Huitema and McKean (1998) have shown, it is also important that the analyst correctly understand that the autocorrelation of concern that must be looked for is in the residuals from the model fitted to the data as opposed to the raw data. The possibility that autocorrelation may cause problems in the analysis of data from single case design studies must be carefully and properly considered, and tests for autocorrelation need to be conducted as a part of the analysis of single case design data.

As the foregoing clearly shows, there can be complex autocorrelation patterns in a time series, and the accurate identification of these patterns requires a relatively long time series. Single case designs used in both practice evaluation and research almost always have relatively few observations, especially by the standards required for the ARIMA methods discussed previously. Hence, the identification of autocorrelation structures in the residuals from the models fitted to the data will suffer from extremely low power. The number of lags that can be employed in autocorrelation and partial autocorrelation functions with short times series is limited, making it difficult to diagnose autoregressive and moving average processes. The short time series seen in many single case designs can profitably be thought of as being part of a much longer time series, and hence viewed as having substantial amounts of missing data. Thus, any identification of autocorrelation in a short time series is at best extremely tentative and laden with the possibility of error.

There are other problems inherent in the analysis of short time series. First, a single data point can exert a significant influence on statistical analyses and visual displays of data. The problems that "unusual" data points—unusual in the sense that they deviate substantially from the others in a phase—pose for statistical analyses have been discussed by numerous authors (e.g., Cohen et al., 2003; Neter et al., 1983). Statistics such as the mean and standard deviation are sensitive to unusual values of data points. The correlation between two variables can be sensitive and unduly influenced by a single unusual data point, and this is especially so in small data sets. Hence, any statistical methodology based on means, standard deviations, and correlations can lead to results that are highly sensitive to the presence of a single unusual data point.

One implication of this sensitivity is that the risk of overfitting statistical models—that is, including unnecessary terms, such as one representing a change in level—to single case design data will be greater with a short time series. While the regression discontinuity model in equation 2.1 is conceptually appealing for the A/B transition and elaborations of this model appealing for more complex designs, there is a significant risk that fitting these models to short time series can lead to misleading hints of autocorrelation in the residuals, as was seen in the previous illustrative analysis. A misspecified model can produce erroneous results, as well as residuals that suggest some form of autocorrelation (Huitema & McKean, 1998). It is also difficult to adequately test the assumptions upon which the statistical models are based with short time series. The data analyst must keep this in mind when analyzing short times series.

Unusual data points in a short time series can also "catch the eye" and potentially mislead the analyst doing a visual analysis. Indeed, unusual data points might "interact" with unspoken assumptions held by a visual analyst, as well as with theoretical and/or other allegiances, to produce erroneous inferences about change (or the lack thereof). For example, consider the hypothetical data in Figure 2.32. The first six data points are strongly suggestive of a slight decreasing trend in the frequency with which Johnny yells as his mother. However, the last phase data point reveals a significant spike in the frequency of this behavior that rises to a level three times greater than the level at any other point in the phase. This single data point changes the decreasing trend shown by the remaining six phase data points into an increasing overall linear

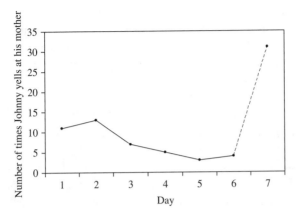

Figure 2.32 Hypothetical single case design phase data with an unusual phase data point at the end of the phase.

trend. This single data point could be very influential in either a visual or statistical analysis.

Now suppose that this final phase data point was taken on a day when Johnny and his mother had a rare argument about doing his homework, during which Johnny became unusually angry at his mother and yelled accordingly. This information would clearly convey to the data analyst that this data point should be viewed in a special manner and perhaps weighted less than the other phase data points. If this information is not known to the analyst, however, and the data point weighted equally with all of the others, then the results of a visual or statistical analysis could be misleading.

This emphasizes another important issue in the analysis of time series data, and especially the analysis of data from short time series, that of *missing information*. If the analyst knew that the final phase data point was associated with an unusual event, perhaps by having this data point marked with a critical incident notation (Nugent et al., 2001; also see Chapter 1), then the appropriate weighting of this point relative to the others could be considered and made by the analyst. However, if the analyst is ignorant about the unusual event associated with this data point, then he or she will be missing important information that would be critical in properly analyzing the short time series. It is probably an axiom of data analysis that the analyst is always ignorant about important factors influencing the level of the dependent variable at different time points. This makes it important that the analyst keep in mind that he or she is most likely missing important information concerning the dependent variable at different time points and therefore must carefully consider the influence of unusual data points on the analytic methods he or she is using. This missing information will take on greater importance the shorter the time series is.

Another issue is that of *missing data*. The short time series the analyst has on hand can readily and profitably be viewed as just a small section from a much longer time series that could, in principle, have been obtained, but that is unavailable to the analyst. This emphasizes the fact that the analyst is working in an environment of missing data, even if none are missing over the time period the analyst actually has data for. For example, the baseline phase data in Figure 1.2 showing six daily measures of the severity of a client's problem with panic attacks can be viewed as just six observations from a time series showing the client's panic problem over a 1-month period. Viewed in this manner, it becomes clear that there are a lot of missing data on the patterns of the client's problem. This can be seen in Figure 2.33, in which a month-long baseline series shows 3 weeks of missing data. Similarly, the seven daily observations of the client's panic problem comprising the treatment phase in Figure 1.2 are a small portion of the data that would be obtained

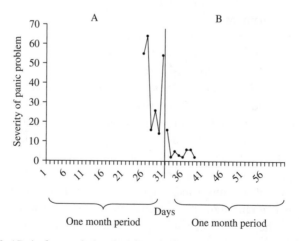

Figure 2.33 AB single case design data from Figure 1.2 but with "missing" data from baseline and treatment phases represented by longer baseline and treatment phase periods.

if the client's problem were observed each day for a month during, and perhaps after, treatment. Again it becomes clear that the short treatment phase time series is a small portion of a longer time series. This is again shown in Figure 2.33, in which the treatment phase shows 3 weeks of missing data subsequent to the last treatment phase measure. The data analyst must keep this in mind when analyzing the data from single case designs. The data patterns in Figure 2.33 may look a bit different from those in Figure 1.2 because of the large regions of missing data.

This highlights a problem that permeates the topic of the statistical analysis of single case design data: *In any data analysis method used, the analyst must contend with the small—perhaps very small—number of data points.* Unless the analyst is willing to make strong assumptions, this small n analysis context will make any statistical analysis challenging. Further, even if the analyst is willing to make rather strong assumptions about the short time series, the small number of observations in most single case designs will make it very difficult to test the validity of the assumptions being made. Thus, the statistical analysis of single case design data is an endeavor that is in most (if not all) cases fraught with significant challenges and risks.

Finally, there are a number of graphical aids that have been advocated as a means of facilitating the analysis of data from single case design studies. Many of these will be considered in subsequent chapters. These methods, too, will be vulnerable to the problems discussed previously that are brought on by the small numbers of observations typically found in single case design research.

STRENGTHS AND LIMITATIONS OF ARIMA AND REGRESSION-DISCONTINUITY MODELS

A major advantage to the ARIMA models is the ability of these models to represent complex patterns of autocorrelation in time series data. A related advantage is the assumption of stationarity. This assumption can be seen as a form of stability. A stationary baseline time series, then, serves as the basis for relatively strong inferences concerning random variation and change across phases. Thus, the risk of the overinterpretation of noise as signal is low. A stationary baseline time series therefore serves as an excellent foil against which to compare and contrast the data patterns in an adjacent treatment phase. The stationary time series also serves as an excellent conceptual model of stability for the single case design data analyst to use when contemplating the implications of the data in a single case design phase.

The most significant limitation of the ARIMA models is the need for a large number of data points. In many, if not most, applied contexts the acquisition of 50 or more data points per phase will not be possible. The regression-discontinuity models, when the numbers of data points are the same as needed for the ARIMA models, have considerable utility. If the data in a long time series are trending in a linear manner, then either first differencing can be used to make the time series stationary or a form of model 2.1 may be used concomitant with ARIMA modeling of the residuals. Thus, the more general regression-discontinuity model shares many of the same advantages as the ARIMA model discussed earlier when the time series is long.

The regression-discontinuity model used with short interrupted time series has the advantage of conceptual appeal, as the analyst can model changes in level and trend across the single case design phase transition. Tests of statistical significance can also be used to help reduce problems with interrater agreement, as found in visual analysis procedures. The regression-discontinuity model used with short interrupted time series has numerous and significant disadvantages, however. The use of these models with short interrupted time series designs runs the considerable risk of the overinterpretation of random variation in much the same manner as in the use of visual analysis methods. The application of a formal statistical model that is an *incorrect model* for the data can lead to erroneous inferences. One consequence of use of an incorrect model for the single case data is type I error since the statistical model can, in a sense, interact with the small numbers of data points to produce statistically significant results that are nothing more than the end result of the poorly fit model. This is illustrated and discussed in Chapter 5 (see Figures 5.9 through 5.11 and associated discussion). There will also be a problem with type II errors due to low statistical power, although this may be seen as an advantage in much the same sense it is viewed as an advantage of visual analysis methods. It will also be difficult if not impossible to adequately test the plausibility of the assumptions upon which the statistical model is based.

3

Graphical and Statistical Methods

In this chapter a variety of graphical and statistical methods will be described that can be used to aid in the visual analysis of single case data. These include graphical methods for representing phase means, trends, and variability. Combined graphical and statistical methodologies for making inferences about change are also described.

GRAPHICAL AND STATISTICAL METHODS OF REPRESENTATION

There are a variety of graphical and statistical methods that can be used to represent various characteristics of single case design phase data. The ones considered here are phase mean and median lines, and methods for representing phase trend, variability, and overlap

Phase Mean and Median Lines

A simple way of graphically representing the mean level of the dependent variable in a single case design phase is to draw a line across a phase that marks the mean of the data in the phase. The phase mean will be unaffected by autocorrelation (Ostrom, 1990). Phase means were shown in various figures in earlier chapters. For example, in Figure 3.1, the means

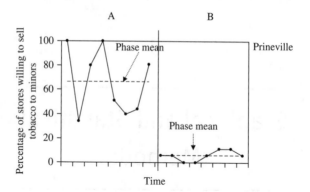

Figure 3.1 Prineville single case design data, from Biglan, Ary, and Wagenaar (2000), with phase mean lines drawn in. Reproduced with kind permission from Springer Science+Business Media. Biglan, A., Ary, D., & Wagenaar, A. (2000). The value of interrupted time-series experiments for community intervention research. *Prevention Science, 1*(1), 38, Figure 3.

of the data in the phases of the single case design study of Prineville, from the Biglan, Ary, and Wagenaar (2000) study, are drawn with dashed lines. Lines can also be drawn representing the median of the data in the single case phases, as shown in Figure 3.2. The median line may be preferable to the mean in cases in which there are extreme values of the dependent variable relative to other values in the phase since the median is less sensitive to extreme values (Pagano, 2006). In the case of the Prineville data, there is little difference between the mean and median lines.

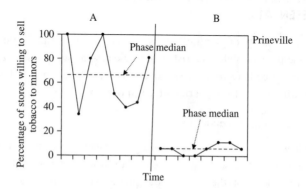

Figure 3.2 Prineville single case design data, from Biglan, Ary, and Wagenaar (2000), with phase median lines drawn in.

Phase Linear Trend

There are at least three approaches to representing linear trend across a phase: the use of an *ordinary least squares (OLS) regression line*, a method described by Nugent (2000) for *hand-drawing a linear trend line*, and a technique called the *celeration line technique*, or sometimes the *split-middle technique* (Bloom, Fischer, & Orme, 2008).

OLS Trend Lines.   Least squares regression methods may be used to compute a phase linear trend equation and then to represent this trend graphically by drawing an OLS trend line, or arrow, through the phase. This estimate will be unbiased even in the presence of autocorrelation (Ostrom, 1990). An OLS trend line is shown in Figure 3.3. This line can be placed simply by computing an OLS regression linear trend equation for the phase data and then using this equation to plot the linear trend line.

Mean Trend Line.   Nugent (2000) described a procedure for drawing in the mean trend line for a single case design phase. Nugent (2000) showed that the trend line created by this method is the weighted—by length of time interval—mean phase linear trend. In this procedure, the trend across a longer interval of time is weighted more than the trends across

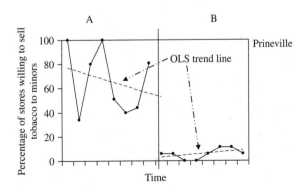

Figure 3.3 Graphic representation of phase trends using ordinary least squares (OLS) regression lines for Prineville data from Biglan, Ary, and Wagenaar (2000).

shorter intervals. This method is simple, and involves nothing more than starting the trend line at the first data point in the phase and then drawing a line or arrow though the final phase data point. In a variation on this method, the mean trend line so created is "slid" until it bisects the phase data points such that the same numbers of points are above and below the trend line. This method is analogous to the hand-drawn phase median line using the method of Ma (2006), and may create a trend line facilitating a better representation of phase variability than the Nugent (2000) method, as discussed later. These methods are illustrated in Figure 3.4 for data from Biglan et al. (2000).

Celeration Line.   This procedure will be illustrated by drawing in a celeration line for the baseline data from the Prineville community data. The first step is to divide the baseline data into two halves, as shown in Figure 3.5. This midpoint line divides the baseline phase into two equal parts. If there had been nine data points instead of eight, the midpoint line would have gone through the fifth data point. In cases in which the number of baseline observations is odd, the midpoint line will go through the data point that has an equal number of data points on either side of it. In cases in which the number of data points is even, such as in Figure 3.5, the midpoint line will divide the phase into two sections with equal numbers of data points.

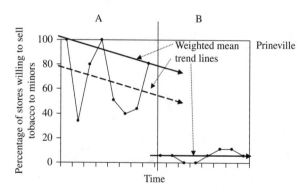

Figure 3.4 Weighted mean trend lines drawn in Prineville data from Biglan, Ary, and Wagenaar (2000). The dashed arrow is the translated trend line bisecting data points in phase.

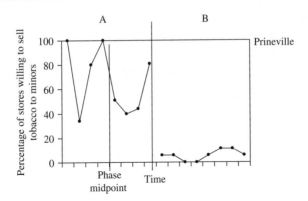

Figure 3.5 Baseline phase midpoint line drawn in to Prineville data from Biglan, Ary, and Wagenaar (2000).

The next step is to draw in lines that further subdivide the phase into quarters, as in Figure 3.6. There will now be lines at the first, second, and third quarter points in the baseline phase, as can be seen in Figure 3.6.

The next step is to compute the mean scores for the first half of the phase and mark that point on the first quarter line, and compute the mean score in the second half of the phase and mark that point on the

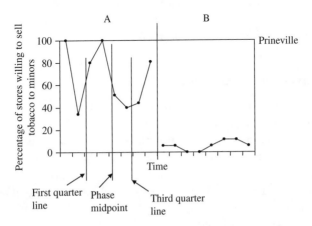

Figure 3.6 First, second, and third quarter lines for baseline phase from the Prineville community data from Biglan, Ary, and Wagenaar (2000).

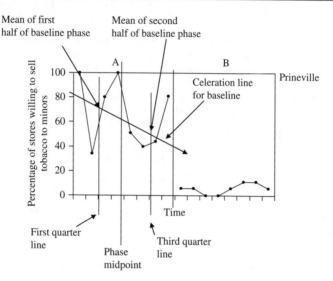

Figure 3.7 Celeration line for baseline phase data from Prineville community from Biglan, Ary, and Wagenaar (2000) study.

third quarter line. Finally, connect these points on the first and third quarter lines with a line. This line is the *celeration line* and represents the linear trend in the data across the phase. The celeration line for the baseline phase in the Prineville data is shown in Figure 3.7. The trend representations based on all four methods are shown in Figure 3.8 for the Prineville data from Biglan et al. (2000).

Representation of Variability

There are a number of ways to represent the variability of the dependent variable across a single case design phase. One is to represent the range of values of the dependent variable using lines marking the upper and lower limits of the range of values across the phase, as shown in Figure 3.9. The dashed horizontal lines mark the upper and lower limits of the range of values of the dependent variable across the phase, while the difference between these lines represents the overall range of values of the dependent variable across the phase.

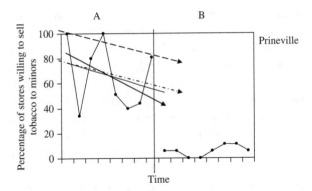

Figure 3.8 Four linear trend representations for Prineville baseline data from Biglan, Ary, and Wagenaar (2000). Upper dashed arrow is based on Nugent (2000) method. Solid line is ordinary least squares (OLS) regression trend line. Solid arrow is celeration line, while lower dashed arrow is Nugent method mean trend line "slid" so as to bisect phase data points.

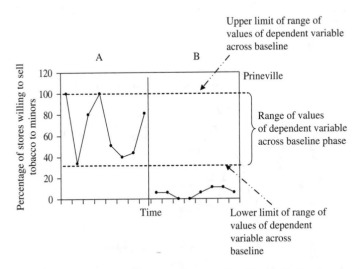

Figure 3.9 Illustration of use of lines marking upper and lower limits of range of values of dependent variable during a baseline phase using Prineville data from Biglan, Ary, and Wagenaar (2000) study.

Lines can also be used to represent such measures of dispersion across a phase as the standard deviation and the interquartile range. Methods for computing these statistics can be found in such sources as Pagano (2006). An example of standard deviation and interquartile range lines are illustrated in the graphs in Figures 3.10 and 3.11 for the Prineville data from Biglan et al. (2000). Lines marking one standard deviation above and below the phase mean are shown in Figure 3.10. Lines marking two standard deviations above and below the phase mean line have been advocated as a part of a procedure for making inferences about change (Nourbakhsh & Ottenbacher, 1994).

Lines marking the first and third quartile scores for the phase are shown in Figure 3.11, along with a line marking the median (second quartile) score. The distance between the first and third quartile scores marks the interquartile range for phase observations. One advantage of using the median and interquartile range to represent characteristics of single case design phase data is that these statistics are less sensitive to extreme scores than are the mean and the standard deviation (Pagano, 2006). Hence, the median and interquartile range may be more robust for representing the central tendency and variability, respectively, of the data in a single case design phase.

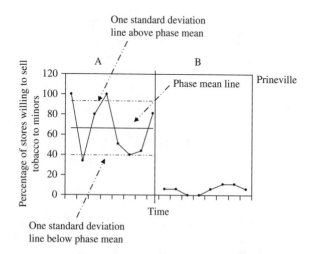

Figure 3.10 Illustration of lines marking one standard deviation above and below the phase mean lines in Prineville data from Biglan, Ary, and Wagenaar (2000).

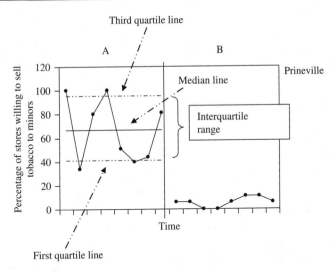

Figure 3.11 Illustration of graphic representation of interquartile range using Prineville data from Biglan, Ary, and Wagenaar (2000).

Another method of representing variability is the *average, or mean, moving range*, a method used in statistical process control (Orme & Cox, 2001; Pfadt & Wheeler, 1995; Wheeler, 1995). °The moving range is defined as the absolute value of the difference between two successive data points in a single case design phase, $|Y_t - Y_{t+1}|$, where Y_t is the phase observation at time t and Y_{t+1} is the observation at time $t+1$. The mean moving range, $\overline{mR}$, is the mean of these moving range values. For example, suppose that the values of the observations in a phase are 4, 6, 2, 7, and 1. The moving range for the first two data points is $|4 - 6| = 2$; for the next two data points, 4; for the next two data points, 5; and for the last two data points, 6. Hence, the mean moving range is,

$$\overline{mR} = \frac{2 + 4 + 5 + 6}{4} = 4.25.$$

Note that if there are n data points in a phase, there will be $n–1$ moving range values for the phase.

The mean moving range can be used to compute the *sigma unit*, an index that can also be used to represent variability (Orme & Cox, 2000; Pfadt & Wheeler, 1995; Wheeler, 1995). Following Wheeler and

Chambers (1992), three sigma units will be given by $2.66 \times \overline{mR}$; two sigma units by $(2/3) \times 2.66\overline{mR}$; and one sigma unit by $(2.66/3) \times \overline{mR}$. One, two, and three sigma lines can be placed above and below the phase mean line to represent variability. A method by which one, two, and three sigma bands can be placed around a phase linear trend line is illustrated later.

Representing Background Variability

Background Variability Relative to Mean.   Single case design methodologists who have advocated the visual analysis of single case design data have argued that treatment phase data should be contrasted against the "background variability" of the baseline phase data (Barlow, Hayes, & Nelson, 1984; Kazdin, 1982; Parsonson & Baer, 1986). Nourbakhsh and Ottenbacher (1994) operationalized this approach by placing lines marking two standard deviations above and below the phase mean line, as illustrated in their Figure 2 (p. 774) and outlined in Table 1 (p. 771) in their 1994 article. A similar method for representing baseline phase background variability is adapted from statistical process control and involves placing one, two, and three sigma bands above and below a baseline phase mean line extended into treatment phase (Orme & Cox, 2001; Pfadt & Wheeler, 1995). This methodology is described and illustrated below.

Methods such as the two-standard deviation band procedure are problematic in that they neglect linear trend. This issue was illustrated by Nourbakhsh and Ottenbacher (1994) in the contrast between parts (a) and (b) in their Figure 2 (p. 774). A similar contrast is shown in Figure 3.12. The baseline mean line has been extended into and across treatment phase, and the two standard deviation bands for baseline data have been drawn in this figure. Note also in this figure the OLS baseline and treatment phase trend lines (dashed lines) and the OLS trend line for the entire time series (solid line). While the treatment phase data pattern relative to the baseline mean line and the two standard deviation bands is suggestive of change (Nourbakhsh & Ottenbacher, 1994), the congruence of the three trend lines implies that it is very plausible that the treatment phase trend is nothing more than a continuation of the baseline phase trend. Thus, the hints of change based on

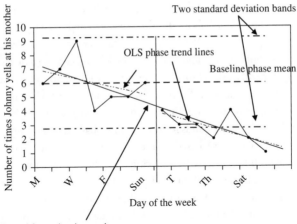

Figure 3.12 Hypothetical AB single case design from Figure 1.2 with baseline mean line, and two standard deviation bands for baseline variability, drawn and extended into treatment phase. Also shown are baseline and treatment phase ordinary least squares (OLS) trend lines and the OLS trend line for entire time series.

comparisons of the treatment phase data with the baseline mean and two standard deviation bands are contradicted by the apparent continuation across treatment phase of a decreasing baseline trend. Ignoring the trend information, and relying solely on the two standard deviation bands representing baseline variability relative to the baseline phase mean line, may therefore lead to erroneous inferences about change between phases. This is an issue similar to that of misspecified statistical models considered later.

Background Variability Relative to Trend.   Nugent (2000) described a method of graphically representing the background variability in a phase *relative to a trend line* as opposed to the mean. This approach was built upon suggestions from Bailey (1984) and Bloom and Fischer (1982, pp. 468–471). A slightly modified version of this procedure, justified in a later section, is carried out as follows and illustrated in Figure 3.13:

(1) Compute the OLS regression model for the baseline linear trend, and then plot the OLS trend line across baseline phase and extend this line into and across the treatment phase, as illustrated in Figure 3.13.

(2) Compute the mean moving range (Wheeler & Chambers, 1992) for the *residuals* about this OLS linear trend line. This is done by (*a*) computing the OLS residuals for the baseline linear trend; (*b*) computing the moving range for each adjacent pair of residuals (this will be the absolute value of the difference between the residual for the data point for time *t* and that for time *t*+1); and (*c*) computing the mean of these moving range values, $\overline{mR}$.

(3) Draw in sigma bands for the baseline phase data relative to the OLS linear trend line based on the mean moving range. The one sigma band lines are drawn by placing lines above and below, and parallel to, the linear trend line a distance $0.887 \times \overline{mR}$ from the trend line. The two sigma band lines are drawn, just as the one sigma bands are, but a distance $1.77 \times \overline{mR}$ from the trend line. The three sigma band lines are drawn a distance $2.66 \times \overline{mR}$ from the OLS trend line (Wheeler & Chambers, 1992). These lines are extended from baseline phase into and across treatment phase.

One, two, and three sigma bands so created can be seen in Figure 3.13. These bands mark the regions of baseline phase background variability *relative to the baseline OLS trend*. The computation of these bands is shown in the next paragraph.

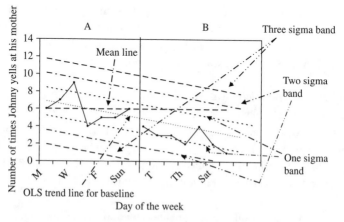

Figure 3.13 Illustration of creation of region of background variability for baseline data from Figure 1.2 using variation of method described by Nugent (2000).

The OLS regression model for baseline data is $y_t = 5.143 - 0.286t$, and the residuals from this OLS trend line are -0.85714; 0.42857; 2.71429; -2.0; -0.71429; -0.42857; and 0.85714. The moving range values are 1.28571; 2.28572; 4.71429; 1.28571; 0.28572; and 1.28571. The mean of these values is 1.857. Hence, the one sigma value is $(2.66/3) \times 1.857$, or 1.6; the two sigma value is 3.3; and the three sigma value is 4.9 (Wheeler & Chambers, 1992). Therefore, the one sigma bands will be above and below, parallel to, and 1.6 units away from the extended OLS baseline trend line. The two sigma bands will be similarly situated 3.3 units away from the baseline linear trend line, while the three sigma bands will be 4.9 units from the extended trend line. These are all shown in Figure 3.13.

COMBINED GRAPHICAL AND STATISTICAL METHODS

No-Trend Models

A Median-Based Method.   Two analytic procedures have been proposed that combine graphical and statistical methods that are based on the notion of overlap, discussed earlier in this chapter and that are based on representing variability relative to the mean or median. One described by Scruggs and Mastropieri (1998) is termed the *percentage of nonoverlapping data (PND)* method. Ma (2006) critiqued this method and suggested an alternative, the *percentage of data points exceeding the median (PEM)*, which addressed limitations identified by Ma in the PND method. The PEM method is implemented as follows:

(1) A median line is drawn across baseline phase and extended into and across the adjacent treatment phase. This could also be done by drawing a median line across a treatment phase and extending it into and across either an adjacent baseline or treatment phase.

(2) The percentage of the data points in the adjacent treatment (or baseline) phase that are above the extended median line if this direction indicates improvement (or below the extended median line if this direction is indicative of improvement) is computed.

(3) The null hypothesis in the PEM approach can be stated loosely as, *if the adjacent treatment (baseline) phase data pattern is a continuation*

> *of the baseline phase data pattern, then 50% of the data points in the adjacent phase should be above the extended median line, and 50% should be below this line* (Ma, 2006).

(4) The greater the percentage of data points on one side of the extended median line, the greater the magnitude of change. If the criteria recommended by Scruggs and Mastropieri (1988) are used, then 90% or more of the data points above (below) the extended baseline median line would imply a large effect; 70% to 90% above (below) the extended median line would indicate moderate change; 50% to 70% would indicate a mild or questionable effect; and 50% would indicate no effect.

This method is illustrated, for the data in Figure 3.13, in Figure 3.14. In this figure, 100% of the data in the treatment phase are below the extended baseline phase median line. On the basis of the PEM method and the criteria of Scruggs and Mastropieri (1988), this would be suggestive of a large magnitude change.

A Method From Statistical Process Control.   A method similar to the PEM, but that is based on statistical process control methods, has been described by Pfadt, Cohen, Sudhalter, Romanczyk, and Wheeler (1992), Pfadt and Wheeler (1995), and Orme and Cox (2001). In this

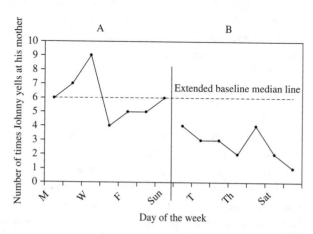

Figure 3.14 Illustration of percentage of data points exceeding the median (PEM) method. Dashed line is extended baseline phase median line.

approach, one, two, and three sigma bands are placed above and below the baseline phase mean line extended into and across the adjacent treatment phase. Then, decision rules, based on the following empirical rules (Wheeler & Chambers, 1992, p. 61), are used to infer change:

(1) Approximately 60% to 70% of data will be located within a distance of one sigma unit on either side of a "mean line."

(2) Approximately 90% to 98% of data points will fall within a distance of two sigma units on either side of a "mean line."

(3) About 99% or more of the data will fall within three sigma units above and below a "mean line."

In this case, the "mean line" is the phase mean line.

Specific decision rules that can be used to decide when the treatment phase data deviate substantially enough to argue that "change" has occurred, relative to the baseline phase, are as follows, again from, and based on, statistical process control (SPC; Wheeler & Chambers, 1992, p. 96):

(1) Any treatment phase data point falling more than three sigma units from the extended baseline mean line indicates a change from the baseline pattern.

(2) Any two of three successive data points that fall on the same side of, and more than two sigma units from, the extended mean line are indicative of change relative to the baseline pattern.

(3) Any four out of five successive data points that fall on the same side of, and more than one sigma unit from, the extended baseline mean line are indicative of change relative to the baseline pattern.

(4) Any eight or more data points falling on the same side of the extended baseline mean line are indicative of change relative to the baseline data patterns.

Wheeler (1995) argues that in a small data context the three sigma rule is especially robust. The small number of data points found in most single case designs would, in most cases, constitute one such small data context.

This method is illustrated for the hypothetical data from Figure 3.14 in Figure 3.15. The lower limits of the one, two, and three sigma bands are drawn in this figure. Note that all seven treatment phase data points

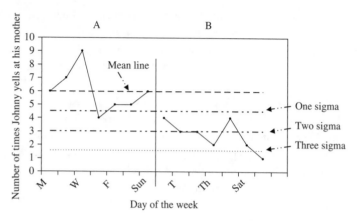

Figure 3.15 Data from Figure 1.2 with lower limits of one, two, and three sigma bands drawn in graph.

fall more than one sigma unit below the extended baseline mean line; two of the last three treatment phase data points fall more than two sigma units below the extended baseline mean line; and the last treatment phase data point lies more than three sigma units below the extended baseline phase mean line. Thus, by rules one, two, and three it can be inferred that change has occurred between baseline and treatment phases.

Lower one and two sigma bands relative to the baseline phase mean line are shown in Figure 3.16 for the Prineville data from the Biglan et al. (2000) study. In this figure it can be seen that all of the eight treatment phase data points are below the mean line and the one sigma bound, and six of eight are below the two sigma bound. By rules two, three, and four listed previously, these treatment phase data patterns are consistent with change between baseline and treatment phases for this community.

Note that in Figure 3.16, a lower three sigma band cannot be drawn in the graph because of a *floor effect* in the measurement of the dependent variable; since scores cannot drop below 0%, a lower three sigma bound cannot be extended below 0%. This highlights a limitation with any of these methods in which background variability is represented graphically and used to infer change: *Floor* and/or *ceiling effects* can make it impossible to set these graphical bounds. This will make it impossible to use some decision rules, such as those listed previously. In such a case the analyst may need to make a case for change sans the use of these decision

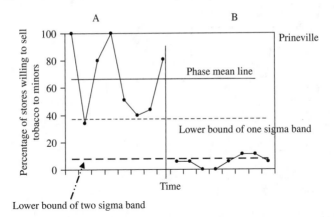

Figure 3.16 One and two sigma bands for Prineville data from Biglan, Ary, and Wagenaar (2000).

rules, with the argument based on how the treatment phase data points contrast with whatever background variability representation is possible.

Trend-Based Models

The aforementioned models assume that there is no baseline trend, so the baseline mean can serve as the reference line for baseline phase background variability. However, if there is a trend in the data across baseline phase, then representing background variability for the phase relative to the phase mean can lead to misleading conclusions about change (Nourbakhsh & Ottenbacher, 1994; Stocks & Williams, 1995). The aforementioned SPC methods can be modified and used relative to a phase mean trend line, along lines suggested by Nugent (2000). The OLS trend line is fitted for baseline data and extended into and across the adjacent treatment phase. Then one, two, and three sigma bands are drawn above and/or below and parallel to this trend line as described previously. Then the decision rules discussed and illustrated previously may be used to infer change, but in this case *relative to the OLS trend line*.

The OLS trend line is a form of mean line (Neter, Wasserman, & Kutner, 1983) that serves in this case as the "mean line" for the sigma bands. Fitting the sigma bands relative to the OLS trend line removes autocorrelation associated with the linear trend of the baseline data

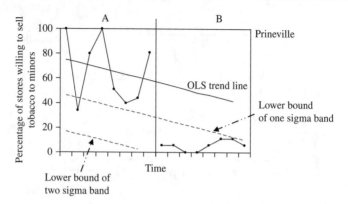

Figure 3.17 Prineville data from Biglan, Ary, and Wagenaar (2000), with ordinary least squares (OLS) baseline trend line and one and two sigma lines below the trend line.

(Huitema & McKean, 1998). Inferences based on the baseline phase background variability relative to the OLS trend line would therefore presumably be expected to be influenced less by this irrelevant autocorrelation. The SPC sigma bands about the OLS trend line for the Prineville data from the Biglan et al. (2000) study can be seen in Figure 3.17. As can be seen in this figure, all eight treatment phase data points are below the trend line and the lower one sigma bound, and none are below the two sigma bound. An inference of change could be made for the treatment phase data on the basis of rules three and four listed previously. Note that the inference of change here is less robust than that relative to the extended baseline mean line since the data patterns (relative to the trend) meet fewer of the SPC criteria for change. This illustrates the findings by such researchers as Nourbakhsh and Ottenbacher (1994), Stocks and Williams (1995), and Huitema and McKean (1998) that the results of the analysis of data from single case designs may vary as a function of the data analytic method used.

Combined No-Trend and Trend Models

The discussion of the no-trend and the trend-based models leads immediately to the question of when one or the other should be used. One approach would be to use the trend-based methods only if the phase trend is statistically significant. This criterion, however, is extremely vulnerable to problems of statistical power given the typically small numbers of data points in a single case design phase. The question of whether a phase trend is "significant" again brings to mind the comments of Parsonson and Baer (1986; p. 167) already quoted in Chapter 1:

> A slow increasing trend in her likelihood to cross the street safely can be seen. In a 8-point baseline, that might be attributed to chance variation; on the other hand, it is visible, and interpretation later will depend on what changes can be seen relative to this baseline. *Thus, it does not really matter whether the baseline is truly increasing; what matters is that any intervention applied after this baseline must produce effects clearly contrasting to it*—and any intervention that cannot produce effects better than that need not be validated as functional, anyway: it will have no use in a pragmatic world (italics added).

Thus, a second approach would be to base the representation of background variability on any apparent trend, as opposed to the phase mean, regardless of whether it is "significant" in some statistical sense.

One problem with this approach is the possibility of misinterpreting random variation as systematic trend, as discussed in Chapter 1. A second problem with this approach is that the apparent trend in a single case design phase can be substantially influenced by a single data point, misleading the analyst as to how the dependent variable is changing across the phase. Consequently, referencing the background variability in a single case design phase on the apparent trend may, in the long run, be as misleading as basing it on a phase mean line.

Given the small numbers of observations in most single case designs, a critical principle of single case design data analysis should be that of *considering alternative models*. Rather than employing in a routine manner a single analytic approach, the analyst would do well to use a variety of models for making inferences about change between phases. One pair of alternative models would be no-trend and trend-based representations of background variability. The analyst could contrast baseline and treatment phase data through the lenses of *both* mean line and trend line representations of baseline background variability. This could be done by analyzing the data from each perspective individually and then making inferences about change on the convergence versus nonconvergence of results from the two perspectives. A second approach would be to analyze the data from the two perspectives *simultaneously* and demand that the results based on both ways of representing background variability lead to the same conclusion. Fisher, Kelly, and Lomas (2003) presented such an analysis approach that makes use of both mean and trend lines for a phase in a single case design.

Figure 3.18 shows the Prineville data from Biglan et al. (2000) with both mean-based and OLS trend-based representations of baseline phase background variability drawn simultaneously on the single case design graph. The analyst using this combined approach could require that the results from contrasting the treatment phase data with *both mean-based and OLS trend-based representations of baseline phase background variability meet one or more of the four SPC decision rules listed previously.* In this case, that requirement is met with respect to decision rules three and four.

This combined approach has the advantage of making irrelevant the issue of whether or not a phase trend is in some way significant. It brings with it, however, the possible ambiguity of conclusions about change when the results differ between the mean-based and OLS trend-based representations of background variability.

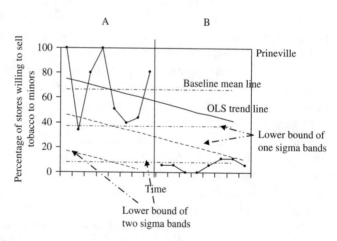

Figure 3.18 Data from Prineville community from Biglan, Ary, and Wagenaar (2000), with mean-based and ordinary least squares (OLS) trend-based representations of baseline phase background variability using statistical process control (SPC) methods and one and two sigma bounds.

This possible disparity in results underscores the findings of researchers such as Nourbakhsh and Ottenbacher (1994) and Stocks and Williams (1995) that suggest that the results of the analysis of single case design data are at least to some extent dependent on the analytic method used, and that different methods can lead to different conclusions about the same single case design data. Perhaps the most reasonable way out of this conundrum is to use multiple methods, considering alternate hypotheses and explanations for the data patterns that emerge from analysis procedures such as those discussed previously. If the results of the multiple and various analytic approaches agree, and alternate explanations can be ruled out, then the researcher or practitioner can have confidence about the conclusions drawn from the analysis. If the results differ, however, as a function of different methods, then the analyst must note this and place the results of the analysis in the proper cautionary context. This form of conditional interpretation of the results of the analysis of the data from single case design studies may be a form of ambiguous conclusion that is not only unavoidable but perhaps also necessary and desirable in order to help avoid overly optimistic conclusions about change and treatment effects. This is one of the consequences of using a methodology that employs interrupted time series designs with small numbers of observations.

A GRAPHICAL METHOD FOR PRACTITIONERS

The aforementioned methods are most appropriate for researchers since they involve the computation of OLS regression equations that are then used to draw in OLS trend lines on single case design phases. Nugent (2000) described and justified a relatively simple graphic procedure that could be used by practitioners to analyze single case design data. A somewhat modified version of that method follows.

First, the mean trend across a baseline (or treatment) phase is plotted by:

(1) Drawing a line or arrow from the first data point in the phase through the last data point in the phase. The average trend across the phase is simply the value of the first data point subtracted from the value of the last data point divided by the length of time between the first and last phase data points. As shown below, the

mean trend across the phase is given by $\frac{Y_{t_f} - Y_{t_i}}{t_f - t_i}$, where Y_{t_f} is the numeric value of the final phase data point, Y_{t_i} the numeric value of the first data point in the phase, t_f is the time that the final phase data point was observed, and t_i the time of the initial data point. A proof is offered in a following section that this procedure actually represents the mean trend.

(2) Then slide the trend line to a location in the phase such that, if possible, there are the same number of data points on either side of it. The goal is to have the trend line as much as possible bisect the phase data points. The trend line is then extended into and across the single case design phase subsequent to this phase.

(3) The phase background variability is then represented as follows. First, find the phase data point *farthest from the mean trend line*. A line is then drawn through this data point, parallel to the mean trend line, and across the phase and into and across the subsequent phase of the single case design. The distance between this line and the mean trend line *is used as an estimate of one sigma unit*. A following section contains proof that this distance is a reasonable estimate of one sigma unit and, on average, slightly overestimates this value.

(4) Then, on the opposite side of the trend line from the line drawn in (3), place a second line across the phase that is the same distance from the trend line as that drawn in (3) and that is parallel to the mean trend line. This line is drawn into and across the subsequent single case design phase. The region spanned between these lines parallel to and on either side of the mean trend line represents the estimated one sigma region of background variability for the phase. The practitioner can then draw in two and three sigma bands based on the estimated one sigma bounds.

The practitioner can then make use of decision rules one through four listed previously to make inferences about change between the phases. If there are too few data points to make use of these rules, then the practitioner can make the best argument possible based on these decision rules (or using alternate decision rules discussed below). In general, the greater the number of data points in the subsequent phase that (*1*) fall on one side of the extended mean trend line and (*2*) fall outside one or more of the extended regions of background variability defined by one, two, and three estimated sigma units, the better the case the practitioner can make that change has occurred between the two phases.

Figure 3.19a shows the Prineville data with the mean trend arrow drawn in by connecting the first and last baseline phase data points, as described previously. Figure 3.19b shows this arrow after moving it downward to an approximate position bisecting the baseline phase data points. Figure 3.20a shows the bottom limit of the one sigma

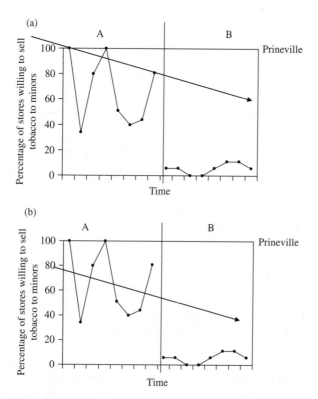

Figure 3.19 (a) Prineville data, from Biglan, Ary, and Wagenaar (2000), with mean baseline trend arrow drawn in using method of Nugent (2000). (b) Prineville data, from Biglan, Ary, and Wagenaar (2000), with mean baseline trend arrow repositioned to bisect baseline data using modification of method of Nugent (2000).

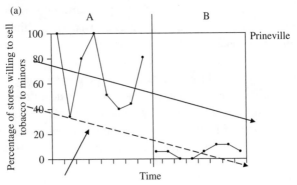

(a)

Line marking bottom limit of approximate
one sigma unitbackground variability

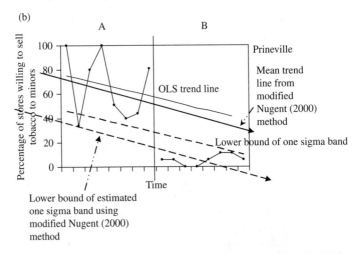

(b)

Lower bound of estimated
one sigma band using
modified Nugent (2000)
method

Figure 3.20 (a) Prineville data, from Biglan, Ary, and Wagenaar (2000), with lower line marking estimate of one sigma unit using modified Nugent (2000) method. (b) Graphic comparison of ordinary least squares (OLS) trend-based and modified Nugent (2000) method-based estimates of one sigma unit.

bound estimated using the aforementioned method. Figure 3.20b shows how this estimate compares with that created using the method described earlier based on the OLS trend line and SPC methods. In this case, the modified Nugent (2000) method overestimates the one sigma bound, and therefore actually gives a more conservative test of an intervention effect.

This methodology will suffer from the same problems discussed previously for the use of any trend-based representation of background variability. The cautious practitioner would do well to analyze his or her single case design data simultaneously using both the trend-based method discussed here and the PEM method described earlier. If the results from both approaches lead to the conclusion that his or her client has experienced change, then the practitioner's conclusion is likely on reasonably good inferential grounds.

PROOF THAT LINE CONNECTING FIRST AND LAST DATA POINTS IN PHASE GIVES MEAN TREND LINE

This proof is based on that of Nugent (2000). The reader may skip this section if he or she would like, especially if such things as proofs are unpalatable. Let Y_i be the value of the dependent variable obtained at time t_i, and let there be n observations of the dependent variable across the single case design phase, so $i = 1, 2, \ldots, n$. The change in the dependent variable between two successive observations will be,

$$\Delta Y_i = Y_{i+1} - Y_i,$$

with $i = 1, 2, \ldots, n-1$. The time interval across which the dependent variable changes by ΔY_i will be,

$$\Delta t_i = t_{i+1} - t_i,$$

with $i = 1, 2, \ldots, n-1$. By definition, the trend of the dependent variable between two successive observations taken at times t_i and t_{i+1} is T_i and is given by,

$$T_i = \frac{\Delta Y_i}{\Delta t_i} = \frac{(Y_{i+1} - Y_i)}{(t_{i+1} - t_i)}.$$

This trend can be defined as the *local mean trend* across the given time interval Δt_i (Gottman, 1981). This local trend gives the OLS trend between the two data points (Neter et al., 1983).

Now the weighted mean trend of the level of the dependent variable across the phase of the single case design is (Ash, 1993),

$$T_m = \frac{\left[\displaystyle\sum_{i=1}^{n-1} w_i T_i\right]}{\left[\displaystyle\sum_{i=1}^{n-1} w_i\right]}$$

where T_i = the local mean trend across interval i, and w_i = the weight given to the local mean trend across the interval i.

One weight that can be used is the time interval Δt_i that a given local mean trend covers. Local mean trends covering longer time intervals should be given greater weight than those covering shorter time intervals. If the time interval Δt_i is used as the weight w_i, then the term in the denominator of the weighted mean trend is the total length of time between the first and last of the phase observations. This follows since,

$$\sum_{i=1}^{n-1} w_i = \sum_{i=1}^{n-1} (t_{i+1} - t_i)$$
$$= (t_2 - t_1) + (t_3 - t_2) + \ldots + (t_n - t_{n-1}) = t_n - t_1.$$

Therefore, the weighted mean trend across the phase will be,

$$T_m = \frac{\left[\displaystyle\sum_{i=1}^{n-1} w_i T_i\right]}{\left[\displaystyle\sum_{i=1}^{n-1} w_i\right]} = \frac{\left[\displaystyle\sum_{i=1}^{n-1} \Delta t_i \left(\frac{\Delta Y_i}{\Delta t_i}\right)\right]}{(t_n - t_1)} = \frac{Y_n - Y_1}{t_n - t_1}.$$

If all of the observations are equally spaced, then this mean will be the simple mean of all of the local mean trends across the phase. Thus, drawing the line connecting the first and last data points in the phase places a mean trend line across the phase, and the difference between the last and first data points divided by the total duration of the phase is the weighted mean trend of the dependent variable across the phase.

PROOF THAT DISTANCE OF POINT FARTHEST FROM TREND LINE IS A REASONABLE ESTIMATE OF ONE SIGMA UNIT

This section can also be skipped without loss of continuity in the chapter. As argued previously, the trend line can be viewed as a natural frame of reference against which to compare data in an adjacent phase (Parsonson & Baer, 1986). It is as if the analyst were "riding on" the trend line and noting how far data points fluctuate away from the trend line, the analyst's frame of reference. This is illustrated (somewhat tongue in cheek) in Figure 3.21, which shows the author "riding a trend line," observing data points at particular "distances" above and below the line. The author will see data points above, below, and/or on the trend line, and the distances the data points are from the trend line will be the value of the residuals from the statistical model used to fit the trend line.

The model used to fit the trend line is a form of "linear filter," which, through the modeling of the trend, allows a representation of variability relative to the trend line (Gottman, 1981). This model also removes the autocorrelation in the raw data associated with the linear trend, as was noted earlier in the discussion of regression-discontinuity models (Huitema & McKean, 1998). Let's therefore consider how a person riding the trend line might estimate one sigma unit for the data within the trend line frame of reference, that is, relative to the mean trend line.

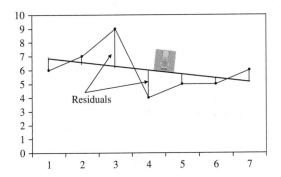

Figure 3.21 The author "riding an ordinary least squares (OLS) trend line," observing data points relative to this trend line as opposed to the frame of reference implied by the single case design graphic.

The residuals relative to the mean trend line—the distance between the trend line and a particular data point—are shown in Figure 3.21. Let the magnitude (i.e., absolute value) of the largest difference (residual) be k. Each residual can therefore be scaled as a function of k by $c_t k$, where c_t is a number ranging from −1 to +1 that scales the residual at time t in terms of the magnitude of the largest residual. The value of c_t is positive if the residual is above the mean trend line and negative if it is below the trend line. If $c_t = -0.5$, for example, it would indicate that the residual was below the trend line and half the magnitude of the largest residual.

The moving range for the residuals at times t and $t+1$ will be,

$$|c_t k - c_{t+1} k| = |c_t - c_{t+1}|k = |\Delta c_t|k,$$

were $\Delta c_t = c_t - c_{t+1}$, for $t = 1,2,\ldots,n{-}1$, and where n is the number of observations in the phase. The values of Δc_t can range from 0 (adjacent data points on same side of, and same distance from, trend line) to 2 (adjacent data points on opposite sides of trend line and each is one k unit from it). The mean moving range relative to the trend line, $\overline{mR}^*$ can be written as,

$$\overline{mR}^* = \frac{|\Delta c_t| + |\Delta c_{t+1}| + \ldots + |\Delta c_{t-1}|}{n-1}k,$$

for i = $1,2,\ldots,n{-}1$. The mean moving range will therefore be,

$$\overline{mR}^* = \left(\frac{1}{n-1}\right)\left[\sum_{t=1}^{n-1}|\Delta c_t|\right]k = \left(\frac{1}{n-1}\right)\left[(n-1)\overline{|\Delta c_t|}\right]k = \overline{|\Delta c_t|}k,$$

with $t = 1,2,\ldots,n{-}1$, and where $\overline{|\Delta c_t|}$ is the mean value of Δc_t. So, the value of one sigma unit will be,

$$\sigma = \left(\frac{2.33}{3}\right)\overline{mR}^* = \left(\frac{2.33}{3}\right)\overline{|\Delta c_t|}k.$$

Hence, k will be, in terms of sigma units,

$$k = \left(\frac{3}{2.33}\right)\frac{1}{\overline{|\Delta c_t|}}\sigma.$$

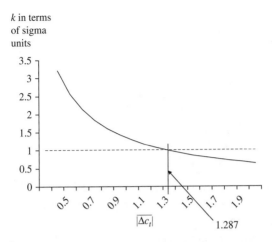

k in terms
of sigma
units

Figure 3.22 Overestimate/underestimate in use of *k* as an estimate of one sigma unit as a function of average value of $|c_t - c_{t+1}|$.

Figure 3.21 shows a plot of *k* in terms of sigma units versus values of $\overline{|\Delta c_t|}$ over the range $\overline{|\Delta c_t|} = 0.4$ to $\overline{|\Delta c_t|} = 2$. The horizontal dashed line shows the point on the vertical axis at which *k* is exactly equal to one sigma unit. As can be seen in Figure 3.22, *k* will be equal to exactly one sigma unit when $\overline{|\Delta c_t|} = 1.287$. Anytime $\overline{|\Delta c_t|} < 1.287$ the use of *k* as an estimate of one sigma unit will *overestimate* this value; contrariwise, if $\overline{|\Delta c_t|} > 1.287$, then the use of *k* as an estimate of one sigma unit will *underestimate* this value. The maximum underestimate will occur when $\overline{|\Delta c_t|} = 2$, and so $k = .64\sigma$, an underestimate of about 36%. The range $0.4 \leq \overline{|\Delta c_t|} \leq 2$ is used in the figure, and in the computations to follow, since it arguably covers the majority of the data found in actual single case designs. The values of $|\Delta c_t|$ that are less than 1.0 would need to range from about 0.06 to 0.3 in the circumstance in which $\overline{|\Delta c_t|} = 0.4$; hence, it seems likely to be the unusual circumstance in which $\overline{|\Delta c_t|} < 0.4$.

The mean value theorem for integrals (Ellis & Gulick, 1986) can be used to find the mean overestimate/underestimate involved when the value of *k* is used as an estimate of one sigma unit *across the interval* $0.4 \leq \overline{|\Delta c_t|} \leq 2.0$. Let's make the substitution $x = \overline{|\Delta c_t|}$. The mean overestimate/underestimate across the range of values of $\overline{|\Delta c_t|}$ from 0.4 to 2 will be (Ellis & Gulick, 1986),

$$\frac{1}{2 - .4} \int_{.4}^{2} \left(\frac{3}{2.33} \right) \frac{1}{x} \sigma dx = \frac{3\sigma}{1.6 \times 2.33} \int_{.4}^{2} \frac{1}{x} dx$$

$$= \frac{3\sigma}{3.728} \left[\ln x \right]_{.4}^{2} = \frac{3\sigma}{3.728} \left[\ln 2 - \ln .4 \right]$$

$$= 1.3\sigma.$$

Thus, the use of k as an estimate of one sigma unit will on average, across the range of values of $\overline{|\Delta c_t|}$ from 0.4 to 2, *overestimate* the value of one sigma unit by about 30%.

As noted previously, in the worst case scenario, when $\overline{|\Delta c_t|} = 2$, then $k = .64\sigma$, so using k as an estimate of one sigma unit will underestimate one sigma by the maximum value. This will occur when (*1*) all of the phase data points are on alternating sides of and (*2*) are equidistant from the mean trend line. Thus, if the practitioner sees that this condition appears to be met, or comes close to being met, then he or she can use the value 1.5k, as opposed to k, as the estimate of one sigma unit. This would entail drawing the line in step (3) listed previously by finding the data point farthest from the trend line *and then drawing the line parallel to the trend line half again as far from the trend line as is the data point*. This line would represent the one sigma bound and should be fairly robust. Indeed, if the practitioner desired to make this procedure as robust and conservative as possible, he or she could use this procedure for estimating the one sigma bounds in lieu of the procedure as described in step (3). The practitioner would then continue on with the methodology as described.

These results suggest that the use of k, the absolute value of the largest difference between a data point and the mean trend line (i.e., residual), as a "rule of thumb" for estimating one sigma unit, and for representing the region of background variability, is reasonable and will on average overestimate one sigma. It will more likely be an overestimate when larger numbers of data points are on the same side of the trend line. It will underestimate one sigma when the majority of the data points are on opposite sides of and about the same distance from the trend line. Research is needed on this proposed methodology, in particular investigating its type I and type II error properties. The author suspects that type II error rates will be low (and hence power high) when k is used as an estimate of one sigma unit. The author further speculates that type I error rates will be lower when the value 1.5k is used as an estimate of one sigma unit. Type I error rates should be lowest when the three sigma rule [decision rule (1) listed previously] is used. This is especially the case when there are small numbers of data points in the single case design. Type II error rates should be lowest, and power highest, when decisions rules (3) and (4) are used.

ALTERNATE DECISION RULES

The decision rules discussed and illustrated previously for making inferences concerning change between phases of a single case design study are based on statistical process control methodology (Wheeler & Chambers, 1992). The use of this methodology for the analysis of single case design data has been discussed by others (Orme & Cox, 2001; Pfadt et al., 1992; Pfadt & Wheeler, 1995). There are at least two other possible decision rules that might be used.

A method developed by White and Haring (1980) makes use of the celeration line described previously, and then a form of binomial test is used to determine whether or not a case for change can be made. The celeration line from baseline phase is extended into and across the treatment phase. If the treatment trend is nothing but a continuation of the baseline trend, then the number of data points in treatment phase above the trend line should be the same as the number below it (Jones, Weinrott, & Vaught, 1978; Nourbakhsh & Ottenbacher, 1994). A binomial test is then conducted comparing the proportion of data points in treatment phase above and below the trend line in the baseline and treatment phases (Ottenbacher, 1986; White & Haring, 1980). This test could be used in lieu of the four decision rules described and illustrated previously. In this case, the binomial test would be conducted on the numbers of data points above and below the OLS trend line from baseline extended into and across treatment phase. Tables for the binomial test can be found in such sources as White and Haring (1980).

Gottman and Leiblum (1974) described a procedure called the two-standard deviation band method that is based on statistical process control theory. In this approach, a baseline phase mean line is extended into and across treatment phase, and then bands marking two standard deviations for the baseline data above and below this mean line are drawn above and below the mean line and extended into and across treatment phase. They argued that two consecutive data points falling outside this band would be indicative of change. This decision rule might also be used but with the two sigma band centered about the extended OLS baseline phase trend line as opposed to the standard deviation of data points about the trend.

STRENGTHS AND LIMITATIONS OF THE COMBINED GRAPHICAL AND STATISTICAL METHODS

The use of graphical aids may improve interrater agreement about change across single case design phases (Bailey, 1984; Hojem & Ottenbacher, 1988; Johnson & Ottenbacher, 1991; Nourbakhsh & Ottenbacher, 1994; Ottenbacher & Cusick, 1991; Rojahn & Schulze, 1985; White & Haring, 1980). This evidence is not unanimous, however (Normand & Bailey, 2006). Overall, however, the use of graphical aids such as trend lines and lines marking regions of background variability appear to be advantageous, especially if *both mean-based and trend-based representations of baseline phase background variability are used simultaneously.*

A disadvantage of the use of such graphical aids is that they may actually facilitate the interpretation of noise as signal. The use of a trend line, for example, when applied to randomly varying data will visually emphasize the local random fluctuations in a longer time series, sorely tempting the analyst to interpret the apparent trend as genuine systematic change across time in the dependent variable. Similarly, the creation of regions of background variability will be prone to error when random fluctuations are interpreted as representing systematic trend.

One limitation of the procedures described in this chapter for representing trend is that only linear trend is represented. No methods are described in this book for representing nonlinear trend. As discussed previously, the short time series typically found in single case designs makes the representation of linear trend somewhat risky. The representation of nonlinear trend would be even more risky in single case design phases with small numbers of data points. Nugent (2000) has described one approach to representing nonlinear trend.

The combined graphical and statistical methods are conceptually appealing in that the baseline data are explicitly represented and then used, via the extension of the baseline model into the adjacent treatment phase, to forecast what the treatment phase data would look like should the baseline phase data patterns continue on without change. This approach is actually similar to the use of a time series to forecast future events, as will be discussed further in Chapter 5 (see, for example, Ostrom, 1990).

The combined graphical and statistical methods for inferring change all suffer from the same limitations associated with short interrupted time series. When using these methods, the analyst runs the risk of overinterpreting random variation as systematic variation. These approaches can be viewed as forms of time series analysis in which forecasts into treatment phase are made from the model used to represent the baseline time series. Thus, for example, the baseline phase background variability relative to the phase mean extended into treatment phase can be conceptualized as a forecast based on the model used to represent the baseline time series. Since this model will in all likelihood be based on a very small number of data points, the analyst will be vulnerable to interpreting local random variation as indicating stability in the sense of a constant mean level of the dependent variable across the phase when, in fact, there is a systematic trend missed by the analyst merely because there are not enough data points for the analyst to detect the trend. Conversely, the analyst may represent the phase background variability relative to an apparent trend and yet be mistaken simply because he or she does not have enough data to detect the stability in level that appears when the longer time series is available. The small numbers of phase data points will also make it very difficult, if not impossible, to discern whether a mean line representation or a trend-based representation is most appropriate. The combined use of mean-referenced and trend-referenced representations of background variability, as described earlier, appears to be the best way of addressing these problems associated with the use only of a mean-based, or only a trend-based, representation of background variability.

The decision rules based on statistical process control (Wheeler, 1995; Woodall, 2000), the binomial test (Nourbakhsh & Ottenbacher, 1994), and the two-standard deviation band approach (Gottman & Leiblum, 1974) are based on certain assumptions. The small number of data points in most single case design phases will make it difficult to test the validity of these assumptions.

Finally, the visual analysis methodology for practitioners described by Nugent (2000) may have a high type I error rate (Borckardt, Murphy, Nash, & Shaw, 2004). More research is needed on the procedures described by Nugent (2000), as well as those described here for use by practitioners, regarding type I and type II error rates.

4

The Analysis of Data From Integrated Single Case and Group Designs

---

S ingle case design methodology is a powerful tool for evaluating the effects of the services provided to clients and the effects of interventions. Single case methodology is so useful because it focuses on the individual person or system. Single case design methods provide a picture of how individual persons or systems improve, remain the same, or deteriorate over time (Barlow & Hersen, 1984; Kazdin, 1982). The longitudinal profile of the dependent variable for the individual subject that single case methods provide is perhaps one of the greatest strengths of this methodology. This is illustrated in Figure 4.1. In this figure are four different paths (A through D) which persons' levels of depression, as measured by a scale with scores ranging from 0 to 100—with higher scores indicative of higher levels of depression and vice versa—might take across time in response to a treatment, each starting and ending at the same point. Note that while each path begins and ends at the same level of depression, the paths are quite different. Path A shows an initially slow decrease that accelerates as time goes on. In contrast, path B shows a constant decrease across time. Path C shows a very rapid initial decrease in depression that quickly decelerates to a

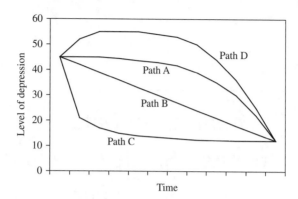

Figure 4.1 Graphic illustration of four different "paths" four different persons' levels of depression take in response to a treatment.

near-constant level. Path D shows an initial increase in level of depression that quickly flattens into a stable level that eventually changes into a rapid and steep decrease. Each of these paths indicates a different treatment response that could be of interest to the researcher or program evaluator. Single case methods allow the researcher or evaluator to study such different treatment response profiles.

The methods of single case design methodology also employ controls over threats to internal validity that allow the researcher to make inferences about the effects of a treatment or intervention *on the specific individual.* This is another tremendous strength of single case methods (Nugent, Sieppert, & Hudson, 2001).

There is another methodology commonly used to evaluate the effects of interventions and programs, that of *group comparison* methodology (Kazdin, 1982, 2003). Group comparison methodology employs controls over threats to internal validity that allow inferences of causality to be made at the level of the group. Matching and random assignment can be used, along with methods such as keeping the researcher and the subjects of the research blind as to the treatment the subjects are receiving, the research hypothesis, and other aspects of the research in an effort to control a host of biases and threats to internal validity. These are great strengths of group comparison studies.

Each methodology, however, has important limitations. For example, it is difficult to generalize the results from single case studies, and single case methods have limited ability to control threats to internal validity at the level of a group of subjects (Kazdin, 1982). Group designs, in contrast, fail to provide detailed information on the response profiles of specific individuals (Barlow & Hersen, 1984; Kazdin, 1982). Group comparison studies usually (though not always) make use of observations of the dependent variable at only one or two points in time. For example, the randomized pretest-posttest design is a group comparison design frequently used in outcome research (Kazdin, 2003). This design employs only two observations of the dependent variable, one prior to treatment and one after treatment. This form of design, then, would entirely miss the different response paths seen in Figure 4.1. The researcher would find that the four persons whose longitudinal response profiles are paths A through D have the exact same initial level of depression and the exact same final level of depression, and would therefore be tempted to conclude that each had the exact same response to the treatment, which of course is incorrect. This is a major limitation of group comparison methodology.

While these two methodologies each have numerous strengths and limitations, as pointed out by many authors (e.g., Barlow & Hersen, 1984; Kazdin, 1982, 2003; Nugent, 1996), they can be used to complement one another. The strengths of one can be used to address the limitations of the other. Thus, combining single case and group methods creates a methodology for studying the effects of programs, treatments, and interventions that can be very flexible and powerful (Benbenishty, 1988; Nugent, 1987, 1996; Nugent et al., 2001). A methodological principal that is critical to any scientific endeavor provides a conceptual link between these two methodologies, that of *replication*.

REPLICATION SERIES OF SINGLE CASE DESIGNS: A CONCEPTUAL LINKAGE OF METHODOLOGIES

Replication is a critically important activity in science, especially in the social sciences (Kazdin, 2003; Sidman, 1960). Replication concerns the ability to duplicate the findings about the effects of a particular intervention used to treat a specific problem. The ability to successfully reproduce the original outcomes serves to demonstrate that the original findings were not a fluke and help form a basis for generalizing the results to other persons, settings, and so forth (Barlow & Hersen, 1984; Kazdin, 1982). The more times a treatment outcome is replicated, the stronger the evidence that the treatment outcome may be expected when using the intervention to treat the same problem with a new person who is similar to the persons involved in the previous successful replications. Under certain circumstances, successful replications can increase the confidence with which one can infer that an intervention under investigation was actually responsible for the successfully replicated outcomes (Barlow, Hayes, & Nelson, 1984; Barlow & Hersen, 1984; Kazdin, 1981).

Replication is important in single case methodology (Barlow & Hersen, 1984; Kazdin, 1982; Sidman, 1960). It is impossible to generalize from a single case, and this inability has been noted as a major limitation in single case design methodology (Barlow & Hersen, 1984). However, the successful replication of single case design results can provide a basis for the generalization of those results (Barlow et al., 1984; Johnston & Pennypacker, 1980). An excellent example of a replication history providing a basis for the applicability of an intervention is given by Johnston and Pennypacker (1980) for the "time-out" procedure. Three forms of replication exist in single case design methodology: *direct replication*, *systematic replication*, and *clinical replication*.

Direct Replication

Direct replication is the name given to research in which a specific researcher reproduces previous research on the effects of a particular intervention for a specific problem across different persons. The persons involved in this form of replication are as much alike as possible (Barlow & Hersen, 1984). The purpose of the direct replication series is to demonstrate that in each instance the same outcome is obtained. If the outcomes are the same, then the replications provide a basis for presuming the intervention will have similar effects when used to treat other persons with the same characteristics and with the same problem. The basis for this generalization has been called *logical generalization* (Barlow & Hersen, 1984). The successful direct replication series also demonstrates that the results obtained originally are dependable since the probability is low that the researcher will have the same lucky happenstance of a positive treatment outcome occurring numerous times in a row.

Systematic Replication

Now suppose that a researcher has conducted a series of direct replications of a study of an intervention for a particular problem, and that in each case the same outcome was found. This successful direct replication series would provide compelling evidence that *clients with the same characteristics as those in the replications* benefit as a result of receiving this intervention. The next step would be to study the same intervention but *with persons whose characteristics differ in some way from those involved in the direct replications*. Replications of this type are referred to as *systematic replications*. The researcher systematically changes the characteristics of the persons with whom the intervention is employed. The researcher may also systematically change the characteristics of the treatment setting, the person administering the intervention, or any other important facet of the intervention context. These systematic changes in subject characteristics, treatment setting, change agent, and/ or other treatment context facets are made in an effort to demonstrate that the same results are obtained across a range of contexts. If the researcher is able to show that the same results can be expected with different clients, different change agents, in different settings, and so forth, then the results are invariant across these different context facet combinations and so, on the basis of logical generalization, are presumed to be likely to be obtained with new clients, in different settings, and so forth.

Clinical Replication

Clinical replication refers to the process in which a clinician *in a practice setting* replicates the use of a specific intervention for a specific problem with several different clients (Barlow et al., 1984). The set of evaluations of the effects of the intervention with these different clients is called a *clinical replication series*. This type of replication fits very nicely within the practice setting. The practitioner simply employs the same intervention procedure with clients who have the same problem and uses a single case design to study the effects of the intervention. A lot can be learned from a clinical replication series. The researcher or practitioner not only can learn that the intervention successfully helps clients in a practice setting, but also can provide data to identify moderators of treatment effects. The replication series can also, as discussed previously, provide a logical basis for generalizing the application of a particular intervention for treating a specific problem with clients having certain characteristics. The replication series can therefore provide an empirical basis for treatment selection or matching.

A replication series can also be used to help build a case that an intervention *caused* clients to improve (Barlow et al., 1984; Kazdin, 1981, 1982). This can be done by building a replication series with certain characteristics. First, the series should focus on the application of the same intervention to treat the same client problem. Repeated measures should be obtained before intervention starts as well as during the application of the treatment. Thus, in this context at a minimum an AB single case design should be used with each client in the replication series. The replication series should include a number of clients with rather heterogeneous characteristics. Under these conditions, *if* (1) each client's problem has a history of stability that suggests that it is unlikely to change without some intervention, and (2) there is a clear improvement in each client's problem *immediately* upon implementation of the intervention, then the replication series provides a level of internal validity that may approach that of a controlled experiment (see Barlow et al., 1984; Kazdin, 1981, 1982). Thus, properly conducted and with the right set of findings, the clinical replication series offers an option for a practitioner or researcher to provide evidence that clients have improved *because of* the treatment provided.

Replication series can also be useful in helping determine why some persons improve, why some remain the same, and (unfortunately) why some get worse because of a particular intervention. One way this can be done is through a *failure analysis*. In a failure analysis, the researcher analyzes the cases in a replication series to determine the common characteristics associated with those who improved; those who did not change; and those who deteriorated during treatment. Such an analysis can lead to the identification of client characteristics, therapist characteristics, and/or setting characteristics that make some persons amenable to the treatment and likely to benefit, others less amenable and not likely to benefit, and even others distinctly nonamenable to the treatment and likely to get *worse* when the treatment is used with them. Excellent examples of failure analyses are given by Foa (1979) and Foa et al. (1983).

AGGREGATING SINGLE CASE DESIGN STUDIES USING GROUP COMPARISON METHODS

Replications of single case design studies can play a major role in the development of knowledge about the effects of interventions. A replication series can be thought of as a way of aggregating single case designs, and the use of group comparison methods can be thought of as providing strategies for purposively aggregating single case design evaluations. The various group comparison methods can be used to impose structure on a replication series.

Thus, the researcher can use single case designs to answer questions about individual research subjects, and replicate single case designs to answer questions about groups of research subjects. This complementarity of single case and group designs makes treatment outcome studies integrating single case and group design methods very powerful approaches to treatment outcome research. Table 4.1, based on Table 7.1 from

Table 4.1 The advantages and disadvantages of single case and group comparison methodologies, and how integrated approaches address these limitations

Methodological limitation	How an integrated approach addresses these weaknesses
Single Case Design Limited ability to generalize from the single case	Aggregation of single case designs can be conducted as a direct, clinical, or systematic replication series, providing a basis for generalization Sampling methods, such as simple random sampling, can be used to further establish a basis for generalization
Limited ability to compare effectiveness of different interventions	Sets of single case designs can be aggregated in order to compare the relative effects of different treatments
Limited ability to identify treatment moderators, such as person characteristics or context factors	Statistical methods can be used to find systematic variation in response patterns associated with different subject and/or context factors

Continued

Table 4.1 (Continued)

Methodological limitation	How an integrated approach addresses these weaknesses
No means of controlling threats to internal validity at the level of aggregated single case studies	Random assignment can be used to control threats to internal validity at the level of aggregations of single case studies
Group Designs	
Only one or two measurement occasions, so information on individuals' response profiles missing	Repeated measurement in single case designs provides individual subject response profiles
Provide no information about which individual subjects improved or failed to improve	Response profiles give information on how individual subjects changed (or failed to change) across time
No control over threats to internal validity at the level of the individual subject	Some single case designs provide control over threats to internal validity at the level of the individual subject

Nugent et al. (2001), identifies a number of advantages of using methodological approaches integrating single case and group methods.

ANALYZING DATA FROM INTEGRATED SINGLE CASE AND GROUP COMPARISON DESIGNS

Nugent et al. (2001) discussed in some detail the analysis of data from studies making use of combined single case and group comparison methods. Briefly, such an analysis will involve, firstly, the analysis of the data from each individual single case design using the methods discussed previously. The analysis will also involve group-level analyses of the aggregated single case design data. A very useful approach to such an analysis is the use of multilevel models (Rogosa, Brand, & Zimowski, 1982; Rogosa & Willett, 1985; Ware, 1985; Willett, Ayoub, & Robinson, 1991), such as hierarchical linear models (HLMs; Bryk & Raudenbush, 1992). The use of this statistical methodology with data from aggregated single case designs was discussed in detail by Nugent (1996). The following is based on that previous work.

HIERARCHICAL LINEAR MODELS

Hierarchical linear models allow the researcher to explicitly model the longitudinal response profile of individual persons who are, perhaps, nested within different groups. This form of modeling allows the researcher to not only model individual patterns of response to treatment but also identify correlates of these response profiles. This has been called "growth curve modeling" (Bryk & Raudenbush, 1992; Rogosa & Willett, 1985; Rogosa et al., 1982; Ware, 1985; Willett et al., 1991). This allows the researcher to be able explain why persons' response patterns differ in shape, such as was illustrated in Figure 4.1.

The HLM approach makes use of two (or more) levels of regression model: an individual subject level regression model and a regression model that represents between-subject characteristics, such as the structure of the group comparison design applied to the aggregated single case design studies. The regression coefficients from the individual level regression models represent the shape of the individuals' longitudinal response profiles. The regression model that represents the group comparison structure of the design, or of the aggregated single case data, has, as the dependent variable(s), the regression coefficients from the regression models representing the response profiles of the individual subjects, while the independent variables are between-subjects' factors such as age, gender, type of treatment, treatment setting, and so forth. In this manner, the between-subjects regression model explains the differences in the shape of the individual subjects' response patterns.

Individual Level Regression Models

At the individual subject level it is assumed that the observed value of the dependent variable for person i at time t, Y_{ti}, across a single case design phase is a function of a response curve and a random error term,

$$Y_{ti} = \pi_{0i} + \pi_{1i}a_{ti} + \pi_{2i}a_{ti}^2 + \ldots + \pi_{Pi}a_{ti}^P + e_{ti}, \qquad (4.1)$$

where a_{ti} is a within-subject variable, such as time in treatment, and π_{ni} is response pattern parameter p (i.e., a regression coefficient) for person i associated with a polynomial of order P. This symbolism, which may appear confusing to some, is used here since it corresponds with that seen in Bryk and Raudenbush's (1992) treatment of growth curve modeling using HLM. Its use here will, hopefully, help the reader more easily move from reading this chapter to reading Bryk and Raudenbush (1992). However, equation 4.1 is just a polynomial regression model, which could also be expressed as,

$$Y_{ti} = B_{oi} + B_{1i}X_{ti} + B_{2i}X_{ti}^2 + \ldots + B_{Pi}X_{ti}^P + resid_{ti}.$$

Each person in the aggregated single case design studies is observed on T_i occasions, with the number and spacing of these observations not necessarily the same for each person. These T_i measures produce the response profile for each of the subjects in the single case designs. The regression model in equation 4.1 represents the differently shaped curves for the individual subjects.

For example, the curves in Figure 4.1 would be represented by a quadratic regression model of the form (again using the symbolism of Bryk & Raudenbush, 1992),

$$Y_{ti} = \pi_{0i} + \pi_{1i}a_{ti} + \pi_{2i}a_{ti}^2 + e_{ti}. \tag{4.2}$$

The different values of π_{0i}, π_{1i}, and π_{2i} in this equation for the four different subjects would describe the differences in the response paths shown in Figure 4.1. The term π_{0i} gives the level of the dependent variable at a specific point in time, such as the beginning of treatment, based on a scaling that will depend on how the researcher scales the time variable; π_{1i} gives the linear rate of change—the linear trend—of the dependent variable at a particular time point, again depending on how the time variable is scaled; and π_{2i} gives the rate of change of the linear rate of change—that is, the rate of change of the linear trend—of the dependent variable for subject i.

As an illustration, the following regression models of the form of equation 4.2 represent the response profile curves A through D in Figure 4.1:

A : $Y_t = 40.05 + 3.37t - 0.458t^2 + e_t$
B : $Y_t = 48 - 3t + 0t^2 + e_t$
C : $Y_t = 41.78 - 7.68t + 0.457t^2 + e_t$
D : $Y_t = 37.91 + 7.95t - 0.83t^2 + e_t$

Thus, for example, for subject A the individual regression parameter π_{0i} is 40.05; the individual regression parameter π_{1i} is 3.37; and the individual level regression parameter π_{2i} is -0.458. These regression equations model the shapes of the response curves in Figure 4.1, and the regression parameters in these regression equations carry the information about the differing shapes of the individual subjects' response profiles.

Between-Group Models

The *differences in shape of response profiles* for the persons in the aggregated single case designs will be modeled by a second level regression equation of the form,

$$\pi_{pi} = \beta_{p0} + \beta_{p1}X_{1i} + \beta_{p2}X_{2i} + \ldots + \beta_{pq}X_{qi} + r_p, \tag{4.3}$$

where π_{pi} is an individual level regression parameter from 4.1, X_{qi} is some characteristic of the person's background and/or some characteristic of the treatment or study context, β_{pq} is the effect of X_{qi} on the pth response pattern parameter, and r_p is a random effect with mean of 0. Again, many readers may find this symbolism a bit confusing, but equation 4.3 is just a regression model, with the regression parameters from equation 4.1 as the dependent variables, and between-subjects distinctions (such as age, type of treatment, treatment setting, etc.) as the independent variables. Equation 4.3 could just as readily been expressed as,

$$B_{pi} = C_{p0} + C_{p1}Z_{1i} + C_{p2}Z_{2i} + \ldots + C_{pq}Z_{qi} + resid_p.$$

In model 4.3, the β parameters are interpreted the same as typical regression coefficients, although they are estimated using empirical Bayes methods (Bryk & Raudenbush, 1992). The empirical Bayes estimation procedures used to estimate these parameters integrate both individual and group-level information (Bryk & Raudenbush, 1992). This level 2 regression equation (4.3) models the differences in shapes of the individual subject response profiles as a function of the between-person variables X_{qi}. Thus, the purpose of the combination of models 4.1 and 4.3 might be, for example, to explain why some persons respond in one way to a treatment while other persons respond differently. Bryk and

Raudenbush (1992) discuss the assumptions upon which these two level models are based, and a good conceptual overview of growth curve modeling can be found in Rogosa et al. (1982) and Rogosa and Willett (1985), and an example can be found in Willett et al. (1991).

For example, suppose that the persons whose response curves are shown as paths A and D in Figure 4.1 are men, while those whose paths are B and C are women. This between-subject variable can be represented by a dummy variable X such that $X = 0$ for men and $X = 1$ for women (Neter et al., 1983). The relationship between the shapes of the response paths and gender can be seen in the correlations between the response curve parameters π_{0i}, π_{1i}, and π_{2i} for paths A through D above and the dummy variable X. The correlation between the parameters π_{0i} and X for persons A through D is $+0.79$; the correlation between the parameters π_{1i} and X is -0.92; and the correlation between the parameters π_{2i} and X is $+0.90$. A level 2 regression model of the form 4.3 will make use of this information and will show the relationships between the individual (level 1) regression parameters π_{0i}, π_{1i}, and π_{2i} and the between-subject (level 2) independent variable X, representing gender. The HLM analysis would therefore reveal a relationship between the shape of the individual subjects' response profiles and gender.

AN ILLUSTRATIVE DATA ANALYSIS: THE ASCHER (1981) STUDY

Ascher (1981) compared the effectiveness of graduated exposure (GE) against the effectiveness of paradoxical intention (PI) for treating agoraphobic avoidance. The dependent variable in this study was a subject's score on a behavioral approach test designed around given places and situations avoided by the subject because of agoraphobic anxiety. The scores on the behavioral approach test (BAT) ranged from 0 to 20. A score of 0 indicated that the subject could not leave home at all, while a score of 20 indicated that the subject was able to leave home and travel to specified locations and then remain there until he or she felt comfortable. Ascher (1981) assigned 10 subjects into two groups of five subjects, one group receiving the GE and the second receiving the PI intervention. The subjects in the GE group—call it group A—were studied using a multiple baseline design in which the subjects were given a standard 6-week GE treatment, followed by the PI intervention. These individual designs were A-B1-B2, with B1 = GE and B2 = PI. The subjects in the second group of five—call it group B—were also studied in a multiple baseline design in which the subjects received only the PI intervention. These individual designs were A-B2 designs.

This design is an example of one integrating single case and group comparison methodologies. The group assignment created contrasting baseline/treatment phases between replication series (groups), while a multiple baseline single case design was used to control threats to internal validity at the level of the individual subject. The single case designs from Figures 1 and 2 from Ascher's (1981) study are shown as the single case designs in Figures 4.2 through 4.11.

Ascher (1981) analyzed the data from this study using statistical methods commonly used in group comparison research. The data from each subject's baseline data were merged into a single data point and then the mean baseline phase BAT scores computed for subjects in the two groups (see Table 1, Ascher, 1981, p. 537). The mean baseline phase BAT score for subjects in group A was 2.07, and for group B subjects 2.08, a statistically nonsignificant difference. The BAT scores for the treatment phases were similarly merged and means computed. The mean BAT score for subjects receiving the GE intervention increased

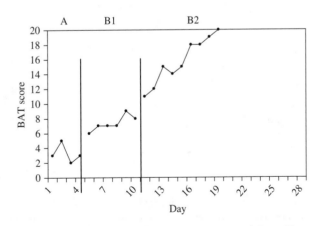

Figure 4.2 Subject number one in graduated exposure (GE) followed by paradoxical intervention (PI) group from Ascher (1981) study. Reprinted from Ascher, L. (1981). Employing paradoxical intention in the treatment of agoraphobia. *Behaviour Research and Therapy, 19*(6), 533–542, with permission from Elsevier.

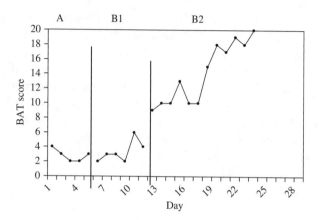

Figure 4.3 Subject number two in graduated exposure (GE) followed by paradoxical intervention (PI) group from Ascher (1981) study. Reprinted from Ascher, L. (1981). Employing paradoxical intention in the treatment of agoraphobia. *Behaviour Research and Therapy, 19*(6), 533–542, with permission from Elsevier.

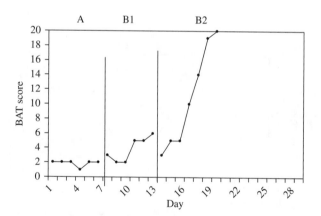

Figure 4.4 Subject number three in graduated exposure (GE) followed by paradoxical intervention (PI) group from Ascher (1981) study. Reprinted from Ascher, L. (1981). Employing paradoxical intention in the treatment of agoraphobia. *Behaviour Research and Therapy, 19*(6), 533–542, with permission from Elsevier.

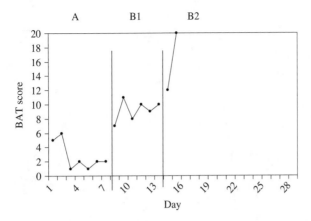

Figure 4.5 Subject number four in graduated exposure (GE) followed by PI group from Ascher (1981) study. Reprinted from Ascher, L. (1981). Employing paradoxical intention in the treatment of agoraphobia. *Behaviour Research and Therapy, 19*(6), 533–542, with permission from Elsevier.

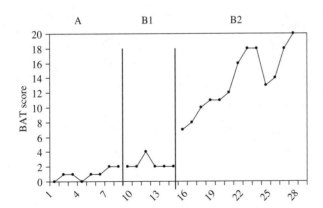

Figure 4.6 Subject number five in graduated exposure (GE) followed by paradoxical intervention (PI) group from Ascher (1981) study. Reprinted from Ascher, L. (1981). Employing paradoxical intention in the treatment of agoraphobia. *Behaviour Research and Therapy, 19*(6), 533–542, with permission from Elsevier.

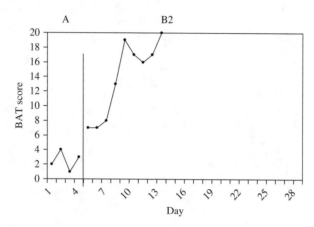

Figure 4.7 Subject number one in paradoxical intervention (PI) group (group B) from Ascher (1981) study. Reprinted from Ascher, L. (1981). Employing paradoxical intention in the treatment of agoraphobia. *Behaviour Research and Therapy, 19*(6), 533–542, with permission from Elsevier.

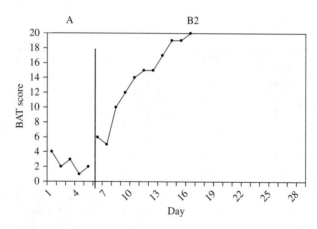

Figure 4.8 Subject number two in paradoxical intervention (PI) group (group B) from Ascher (1981) study. Reprinted from Ascher, L. (1981). Employing paradoxical intention in the treatment of agoraphobia. *Behaviour Research and Therapy, 19*(6), 533–542, with permission from Elsevier.

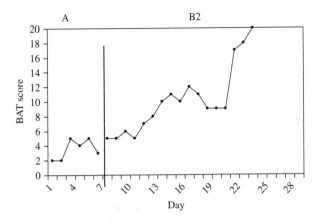

Figure 4.9 Subject number three in paradoxical intervention (PI) group (group B) from Ascher (1981) study. Reprinted from Ascher, L. (1981). Employing paradoxical intention in the treatment of agoraphobia. *Behaviour Research and Therapy, 19*(6), 533–542, with permission from Elsevier.

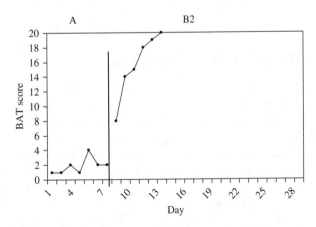

Figure 4.10 Subject number four in paradoxical intervention (PI) group (group B) from Ascher (1981) study. Reprinted from Ascher, L. (1981). Employing paradoxical intention in the treatment of agoraphobia. *Behaviour Research and Therapy, 19*(6), 533–542, with permission from Elsevier.

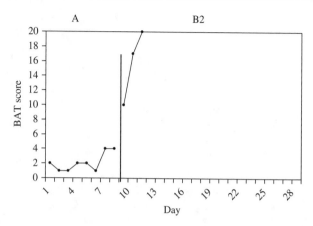

Figure 4.11 Subject number four in paradoxical intervention (PI) group (group B) from Ascher (1981) study. Reprinted from Ascher, L. (1981). Employing paradoxical intention in the treatment of agoraphobia. *Behaviour Research and Therapy, 19*(6), 533–542, with permission from Elsevier.

about 3 BAT units above baseline level $[t(4) = 2.8, p < 0.05]$. The mean BAT score for subjects receiving the PI intervention increased 9.3 BAT units from baseline to treatment phase $[t(4) = 4.4, p < 0.02]$.

An HLM Analysis of the Ascher (1981) Data

Nugent (1996) described an HLM analysis of the Ascher (1981) data. In this analysis the baseline data and the six GE phase measures for each group A subject and the baseline data and first six PI phase BAT scores for each group B subject were analyzed using, for the level 1 model, a regression-discontinuity model as in equation 1.1. The regression-discontinuity model used to represent the baseline and treatment phase data was,

$$Y_{ti} = \pi_{0i} + \pi_{1i}t_i + \pi_{2i}X_{ti} + \pi_{3i}(X_{ti} \times t_i) + e_{ti}, \tag{4.4}$$

where

Y_{ti} = the behavioral approach test score for subject i at time t,
t_i = time of observation for subject i at time t, with time scaled such that $t_i = 0$ for the final baseline phase observation (so the times of the earlier baseline measures were negative),

$X_{ti} = 0$ for baseline (i.e., before the GE or PI treatment started), and
$X_{ti} = 1$ for treatment phase (i.e., after the GE or PI intervention was
initiated).

In this model, the term π_{0i} gives the approach test score at time $t_i = 0$,
that is, at the final baseline observation; π_{1i} gives the baseline linear trend
for person i; π_{2i} gives the change in level of the dependent variable
immediately across the baseline/treatment phase transition; and π_{3i}
gives the change in linear trend from baseline phase to treatment
phase. This model is an example of the regression-discontinuity
models discussed in Chapter 2.

The level 2, or between-subject, model was,

$$\pi_{pi} = \beta_{p0} + \beta_{p1}X_{1i} + r_{pi}, \tag{4.5}$$

where $p = 0,1,2,3$, and $\pi_{pi} =$ the individual response pattern parameters
in equation 4.4, with $p = 0$ for the final baseline level, $p = 1$ for baseline
trend, $p = 2$ for the change in level immediately across the baseline/
treatment phase transition, and $p = 3$ for the change in linear trend from
baseline phase to treatment phase, and where

$X_{ti} =$ a dummy variable representing type of treatment (0 for GE, and
    1 for PI);
$\beta_{p1} =$ the effect of treatment on the pth response pattern parameter;
    and
$r_{pi} =$ a random effect with mean of 0.

This equation models differences in response patterns between individual subjects in Ascher's study, shown in Figures 4.2 through 4.11.

Results.   The HLM model described previously was fitted to the Ascher
(1981) data using the program HLM (Bryk, Raudenbush, Seltzer, &
Congdon, 1988). The results were consistent with the baseline data for
subjects in both groups being equivalent in terms of both level and trend.
The results were also consistent with the immediate changes in level across
the A/B phase transition being equivalent for the two different treatments
$[t(8) = 0.79, p > 0.05]$. The results were also consistent with the distinction
between the two interventions being a statistically significant predictor of

the change in trend from baseline to treatment phase $[t(8) = 3.71, p < 0.01]$. This effect accounted for about 61% of the total variation in change-in-trend parameters across the subjects in the study.

The results were consistent with the change in trend from baseline to PI showing a more rapid improving trend than the change in trend from baseline to GE. Thus, the results of the HLM analysis were consistent with the response profiles for persons receiving the PI intervention being systematically different from those receiving the GE treatment. The persons receiving the PI intervention showed larger increases in linear trend, across the baseline/treatment phase transition, than did the persons receiving the GE intervention. Given the design used, it can therefore be concluded that:

(1) Both GE and PI interventions appeared to cause improvements in subjects' BAT scores.

(2) The PI intervention caused a greater change in agoraphobic avoidance behavior than the GE intervention at the group level. Subjects in the PI group improved significantly more than did the GE subjects.

(3) The effect of the PI intervention appeared to be manifested by a large increase in the rate of subjects' improvement in their ability to enter into places and situations previously avoided because of agoraphobic anxiety. This change in rate of improvement was significantly greater than the rate of improvement manifested by subjects receiving the GE intervention. Thus, the PI intervention appeared to cause a more rapid improvement in the agoraphobic avoidance behavior than did the graduated exposure.

A SECOND ILLUSTRATIVE EXAMPLE: AN EXPERIMENTAL TEST OF THE TENSION REDUCTION THEORY OF ALCOHOL ABUSE

Thyer and Curtis (1984) conducted an experimental test of the tension reduction theory of alcohol abuse. This theory posits that alcohol abuse can occur as a consequence of a person's efforts to self-medicate anxiety by using alcoholic beverages (Conger, 1956). Thyer and Curtis tested a proposition based on this theory that alcohol consumption will cause a decrease in phobic anxiety. This hypothesis was tested by subjecting 22 persons, diagnosable under *Diagnostic and Statistical Manual of Mental Disorders,* third edition (DSM-III; American Psychiatric Association, 1980) criteria as having a simple phobia for a small animal, to a BAT in which the animal for which they were phobic was brought successively closer. During the BAT, the small animal was brought closer through standardized BAT distances until the animal was either in one of several different forms of contact with the subject or until the BAT was terminated due to extreme anxiety on the part of the subject. Subjective anxiety was measured using the Subjective Units of Anxiety (SUDS) scale, on which scores can range from 0 (total calm and relaxation) to 100 (total panic) (Wolpe, 1973).

The 22 subjects first went through a 20-minute resting phase in which SUDS scores were recorded every 2 minutes. This baseline phase provided a non-BAT anxiety response profile for each subject. Each subject then underwent the standardized BAT with the feared animal, with SUDS measures taken at each of the several standard BAT distances. At each standard distance the subject would be asked if it was OK to have the animal moved closer to the next standard BAT distance. If the subject either refused or took more than 30 seconds to give consent for the animal to be brought closer, the BAT was terminated and the subject given the maximum SUDS score of 100 for each remaining BAT distance.

After this first BAT, subjects were randomly assigned in a manner keeping the person conducting the BAT blind as to the group into which the person was assigned. Subjects were assigned into either an ethanol intoxication group (EIG) or a placebo group (PG). Each person in the EIG was given a glass of orange juice with a standardized amount of ethanol alcohol per pound of body weight in it. Each person in the PG was given a glass of orange juice of the same size but with only 7 cm^3 of 100-proof vodka poured on the top. This PG drink mimicked a potent alcoholic beverage and was used in an effort to keep subjects blind as to the group into which they had been assigned.

Each subject then went through a second 20-minute resting phase, with SUDS measures taken every 2 minutes, which allowed the alcohol they had consumed to be metabolized. At the end of this second resting phase each subject's blood alcohol level (BAL) was measured. The BAL of each subject in the PG was 0, while the BAL of subjects in the EIG ranged from 0.05 to 0.16. Subjects then were subjected to the BAT a second time. This second BAT was followed by a final 20-minute resting phase.

As the foregoing describes, each subject in the Thyer and Curtis study was followed at the individual level in an ABACA single case design. The A phases were the resting phases. The B phase was the first BAT, while the C phase was the second BAT the subjects went through, but in this case under the influence of the experimentally manipulated alcohol condition. The A/B phase comparisons allowed assessment of the anxiety provocation during the BATs relative to the resting periods. The comparison of the B and C phase responses allowed a comparison of anxiety response profiles under normal conditions and under the experimentally manipulated alcohol consumption conditions. The comparison of the C phase response profiles between the two groups allowed a comparison of the anxiety response profiles under the ethanol intoxication condition and the placebo condition, and the random assignment of subjects to the two groups provided a level of internal validity such that the inferences based on this comparison of C phases could be about cause-effect. The Thyer and Curtis study is an excellent example of well-designed research integrating single case design and group comparison methods.

A Reanalysis of the Thyer and Curtis Data

Thyer and Curtis (1984) collapsed the response profiles in the various single case design phases, as did Ascher (1981), and then used repeated measures analysis of variance methods to analyze the data. Nugent (1996) used HLM to reanalyze the Thyer and Curtis data. This reanalysis is another example of the use of HLM procedures to analyze the data from research studies employing integrated single case design and group methods. A discussion of this reanalysis follows.

The Individual Subject Level Model

Visual and statistical analyses of individual subjects' B and C phase response profiles in the Thyer and Curtis (1984) data suggested that a quadratic response curve model would best represent these profiles (see Nugent, 1996). Thus, the level 1 model for representing the individual subjects' SUDS score B and C phase response profiles was,

$$Y_{D_k i} = \pi_{0i} + \pi_{1i}(D_k - \overline{D})_i + \pi_{2i}(D_k - \overline{D})_i^2 + e_{D_k i},$$

where $Y_{D_k i}$ = the SUDS score for person i when the feared animal was a distance D_k feet away; and $\overline{D}$ = the mean BAT distance in the phase. The terms $(D_k - \overline{D})_i$ and $(D_k - \overline{D})_i^2$ are "centered" (Bryk & Raudenbush, 1992). This means that they place the distance term D_k into deviation score units. There are a number of advantages of doing this, among them the reduction of problems with collinearity in models with quadratic terms such as the one listed previously (Bryk & Raudenbush, 1992; Neter et al., 1983). Thus, in the previous model the term π_{0i} is subject i's SUDS score at the mean BAT distance from the feared animal; π_{1i} is the linear rate of change (trend) of subject i's SUDS scores at the mean BAT distance from the feared animal; and π_{2i} is the acceleration—the rate of change of the linear trend—of subject i's SUDS scores across the phase (Nugent, 1996).

The level 2 model used to predict the shapes of subjects' SUDS response profiles across the C phase of the Thyer and Curtis experiment was,

$$\pi_{pi2} = \beta_{p0} + \beta_{p1}\pi_{pi1} + \beta_{p2}GP_i + \beta_{p3}BAL_i + r_{pi},$$

where $p = 0,1,2$. In this model, the term π_{pi2} represented one of the three response shape parameters in the level 1 model for the C phase SUDS response profile for subject i; π_{pi1} represented the corresponding level 1 model parameter for the B phase SUDS response profile for subject i; GP_i was a dummy variable (PG = 0, EIG = 1) representing the group into which subject i was assigned; and BAL_i was the blood alcohol level of subject i. This model predicted the C phase SUDS profile for subject i from:

(a) His or her B phase SUDS response profile. The level 2 model parameter β_{p2} gives the relationship between the shape of the C phase response profile and the person's B phase response profile.
(b) The experimental group into which subject i was randomly assigned. The parameter β_{p2} gives the effect of group assignment on the persons' C phase SUDS response profile.
(c) 'The blood alcohol level of subject i when he or she underwent the second BAT. The term β_{p3} gives the relationship between the blood alcohol level of a subject and the shape of his or her second BAT phase SUDS response profile.

As noted by Nugent (1996), the blood alcohol level variable was perfectly correlated with the product term between group assignment and blood alcohol level, and therefore the blood alcohol level variable can be interpreted in a manner similar to that of the interaction between group assignment and blood alcohol level.

Results. The results of fitting this two-level HLM model to the Thyer and Curtis (1984) data are shown in Table 4.2, which is adapted from Table 1 in Nugent (1996). As can be seen in this table, the second BAT response profiles were significantly related to the shapes of the first BAT response profiles, with all three of the second BAT response profile shape parameters related to the corresponding first BAT response profile shape parameter. The shapes of the second BAT response profiles, controlling for the shapes of the first BAT profiles, were also significantly related to group assignment. Specifically, the level and trend of the first BAT SUDS scores at the mean distance of the BAT were significantly related to group assignment after controlling for the shapes of the first BAT response profiles. The subjects' BAL was also related to the shapes of the second

Table 4.2 Final results of HLM analysis of data from Thyer and Curtis experiment

Response profile shape	Parameter	SE	t	p
Intercept parameter	−4.8	6.47	−0.74	0.29
Predictor				
First BAT	0.93	0.10	9.1	<0.01
Group	44.4	13.7	3.2	<0.01
BAL	−531.7	130.9	−4.1	<0.01
Linear trend parameter	−0.25	0.36	−0.69	0.30
Predictor				
First BAT	0.72	0.08	9.0	<0.01
Group	−4.8	1.03	−4.6	<0.01
BAL	39.4	9.6	4.1	<0.01
Quadratic trend parameter	0.03	0.04	0.72	0.30
Predictor				
First BAT	0.73	0.14	5.1	<0.01

BAL, blood alcohol level; BAT, behavioral approach test; HLM, hierarchical linear model. Table based on Table 1 (p. 218) in Nugent (1996).

BAT response profiles, after controlling for first BAT response profile shape and for group assignment.

Figure 2 (p. 219) in Nugent (1996) showed graphically how the shape of the second BAT response profile changed as a function of subjects' group assignment and BAL. These results suggested that the effect of ethanol alcohol intoxication on subjective anxiety depended on blood alcohol level, or more loosely on how intoxicated a subject became as a result of imbibing the alcoholic beverage. Specifically, as blood alcohol level increased, the greater the extent became to which the subject's anxiety during the second BAT was reduced.

ADVANTAGES AND DISADVANTAGES OF USING INTEGRATED SINGLE CASE AND GROUP COMPARISON METHODS

Nugent (1987, 1996) pointed out that the findings from the HLM reanalysis of the Thyer and Curtis data contradicted those of Thyer and Curtis (1984) and were consistent with the tension reduction theory of alcohol abuse. Nugent (1987, 1996) further argued that these contradictory findings came about because of a gain in information from the use of a research design that integrated single case and group comparison methods. Thus, one advantage of integrated methods is that these designs provide information *at both individual subject and group levels that is lost in designs using only one of these methodologies.* Nugent (1987, 1996) concluded that designs integrating single case and group comparison methodologies will likely be superior for evaluating the effects of treatments and interventions to designs using procedures from only one of these methodologies. The use of integrated methods will be especially useful for identifying between-person variables that explain different response profiles found in the evaluation of programs and interventions. These between-person variables may facilitate the optimal matching of treatment with client.

The biggest disadvantage of integrating single case design and group comparison design methodologies is the added complexity. A second and related disadvantage is the additional cost. Research using integrated designs will likely be more expensive not only in terms of money and other resources but also in terms of time.

5

Recommendations

T his chapter will focus on three topics: a conceptual unification of the graphical analysis methods discussed in previous chapters, along with a recommended change to the decision rules based on statistical process control (SPC) discussed in Chapter 3; further consideration of the role that chance can play in the analysis of data from short single case designs; and recommendations for both the analysis of single case design data and future research and development in this area.

AN INTEGRATED VIEW OF GRAPHICAL METHODS

The graphical analysis methods discussed in earlier chapters, especially Chapter 3, can be conceptualized as being based on a statistical model of the general form,

$$Y_t = \text{baseline phase model} + \text{residual}_t,$$

where Y_t is the observation of the dependent variable at time t, and residual$_t$ is the residual from the baseline model at time t. Three specific forms of this model are,

$Y_t =$ baseline mean + residual$_t$;

$Y_t =$ baseline median + residual$_t$; and

$Y_t =$ (initial data point + baseline trend) + residual$_t$,

where the term *initial data point* in the last model refers to a baseline data point with time scaled such that time $= 0$ for that data point, as in the regression-discontinuity models in Chapter 2. The first term on the right-hand side of these models is graphically plotted in the baseline phase. For example, in the mean based model the baseline phase mean is drawn into the baseline phase of the single case design. Then the residual terms from the particular model are used in some specified manner to compute, and represent graphically, the background variability relative to the diagrammatically represented mean, median, or trend of the baseline data, depending on which model is used. These graphical representations are then projected into and across the adjacent treatment phase of the single case design.

Of course, the same forms of models can be used to represent the data from a particular treatment phase and then extended into and across an adjacent baseline or treatment phase, depending on the single case design of interest. The following discussion focuses on baseline/treatment phase transitions, but can be readily applied to treatment/baseline phase transitions, treatment 1/treatment 2 phase transitions, or other such transitions.

ADDING FORECAST ERROR TO GRAPHS

Forecast Error

The extended baseline phase representations into and across the adjacent treatment phase are a form of *forecast* of what the data would do across the treatment phase if nothing occurred to alter the baseline data patterns. These projections can be viewed conceptually as a type of *ex ante forecast* (Ostrom, 1990, pp. 76–90). An ex ante forecast is essentially a prediction of the future behavior of a time series based on how the times series has behaved across a previous time period. In the instance of a single case design, the baseline statistical model is used to forecast what the treatment phase data patterns would likely be if the baseline data patterns continued on without any change into and across the adjacent treatment phase.

An important implication of this conceptualization is that there is an error—called the *forecast error*—associated with such forecasts (Ostrom, 1990). Treatments of time series analysis, such as that of Ostrom (1990) and Box and Jenkins (1976), include explicit consideration of how to estimate such forecast errors. One characteristic of forecast error is that the farther in time an observation is from the data the forecast is based on, the larger the forecast error becomes. Thus, the forecast error for new observations immediately subsequent to the time period the forecast is based on will be smaller, and as the new observations become farther in time removed from the observations the forecast is based on, the forecast error becomes larger and larger. Applied to a single case design, this suggests that if baseline data patterns are used to forecast treatment phase data patterns, under the hypothesis that nothing changes between the two phases, the error associated with this forecast will increase across the duration of the treatment phase.

This is illustrated in Figure 5.1. In this figure the data from the Prineville site of the Biglan, Ary, and Wagenaar (2000) study are shown. Since the model for the baseline data is mean based, a graphic representation of the baseline phase mean and the lower bound of a one

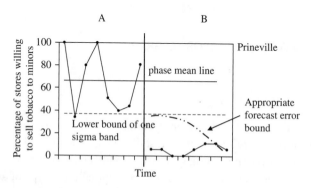

Figure 5.1 Data from Prineville from Biglan, Ary, and Wagenaar (2000), with forecast error bound line for mean-based background variability added into the treatment phase.

sigma band representing the baseline phase background variability are also shown. The baseline phase mean line and the one sigma bound are extended into and across the treatment phase. Also shown is a heavy curving dashed line in treatment phase that illustrates how the error of forecast associated with the region of baseline phase background variability that has been extended into and across the treatment phase might look. Figure 5.2 shows a similar illustration in which the baseline phase model is trend based, while Figure 5.3 shows the same single case design as in Figures 5.1 and 5.2, but with both mean- and linear trend-based representations of baseline data shown simultaneously, along with the curving forecast error bounds added.

While Ostrom (1990) and others have described in detail computational methods for estimating forecast error for time series data, it is unclear at this time how such estimates might be computed for the extended mean-, median-, or trend-based representations of baseline data from single case designs. Thus, the placement of such curves as shown in Figures 5.1 through 5.3 would be, at this point, rather arbitrary. Consequently, while the use of such curves demarking limits of forecast error would be highly desirable and would likely improve upon the graphical methods described in earlier chapters, especially Chapter 3,

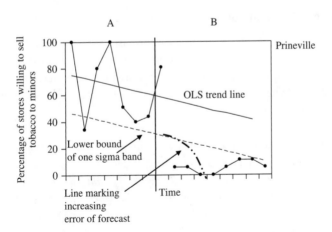

Figure 5.2 Data from Prineville from Biglan, Ary, and Wagenaar (2000), with forecast error bound line for trend-based background variability placed into treatment phase.

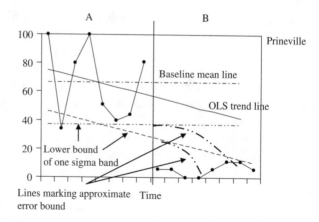

Figure 5.3 Data from Prineville from Biglan, Ary, and Wagenaar (2000), with forecast error bound line for both mean-based and trend-based background variability simultaneously placed into treatment phase.

their use cannot be recommended until methods for computing such curves for the short time series in single case designs are developed. This is one line for future research and development in this area.

Modified Decision Rules

While the use of curves demarking forecast error bounds cannot be recommended at this time, a modification of the decision rules from Chapter 3 can be suggested. These modified decision rules, based on those from Wheeler and Chambers (1992, p. 96), are as follows, with the changes in italics:

(1) Any treatment phase data point falling more than three sigma units from the extended baseline mean (trend) line suggests a change from the baseline pattern. *The closer the data point is in time to the baseline phase data, the stronger the evidence for change, and the farther in time the data point is from baseline, the less strong the evidence.*

(2) Any two of three successive data points that fall on the same side of, and more than two sigma units from, the extended mean (trend) line are suggestive of change relative to the baseline pattern. *The*

closer the data points are in time to the baseline phase data, the stronger the evidence for change, and the farther in time the data points are from baseline, the less strong the evidence.

(3) Any four out of five successive data points that fall on the same side of, and more than one sigma unit from, the extended baseline mean (trend) line are suggestive of change relative to the baseline pattern. *The closer the data points are in time to the baseline phase data, the stronger the evidence for change, and the farther in time the data points are from baseline, the less strong the evidence.*

(4) Any eight or more data points falling on the same side of the extended baseline mean (trend) line are suggestive of change relative to the baseline data patterns. *The closer the data points are in time to the baseline phase data, the stronger the evidence for change, and the farther in time the data points are in time from baseline, the less strong the evidence.*

These modified decision rules may give better type I error control than the comparable rules stated in Chapter 3. This is another area for future research.

THE ROLE OF CHANCE IN SHORT TIME SERIES CONSIDERED AGAIN

As discussed in Chapter 1, the analyst must keep in mind the role that chance can play, visually and statistically, in a short time series. Random variation in the data points in a short time series may easily be over-interpreted as a manifestation of a systematic pattern in the data in a single case design phase. The fewer the data points in the phase, and the larger the variability in the data, the greater the opportunity for chance variation to be erroneously interpreted as a systematic data pattern.

This is illustrated once again, in the interest of emphasis and further explication, in Figures 5.4 through 5.8. A 50-data point baseline is shown in Figure 5.4. These hypothetical baseline data were synthesized by use of the mean-based model, $y_t = 30 + rand_t(0, 5)$, where y_t is the data point at time t, and $rand_t(0,5)$ is a normally distributed random variable with a mean of zero and a standard deviation of 5. The horizontal dashed line in Figure 5.4 is the phase mean of 30. Also shown in this figure are temporal "windows" through which this baseline phase might be viewed in a single

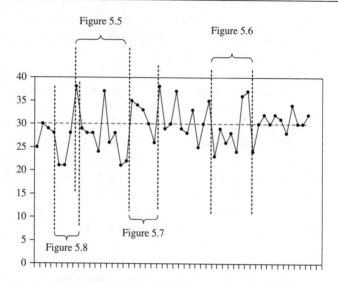

Figure 5.4 A 50-data point baseline modeled around a mean of 30 plus a normally distributed random variable with a standard deviation of five. Identified sets of data points are "windows" through which baselines in Figures 5.4 through 5.8 are based.

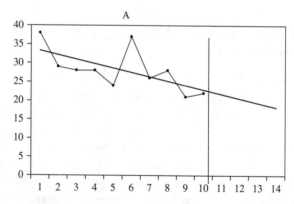

Figure 5.5 A possible baseline of 10 data points pulled from the 50-point baseline in Figure 5.4. Solid line through data points is ordinary least squares (OLS) baseline trend.

case design. Figure 5.5 shows one possible 10-data point baseline phase that could be obtained if circumstances were such that the 10-data point window identified in Figure 5.4 (marked by vertical dashed lines as Figure 5.5) was used to gather the data for the baseline of a single case design. An ordinary least squares (OLS) trend line is also shown in Figure 5.5 for this particular hypothetical baseline phase. There is a fairly clear decreasing trend across this particular baseline. In fact, an OLS regression analysis, with a one-tailed test of the linear trend, would produce statistically significant results, with no evidence of any form of autocorrelation. Viewed within the context of the longer 50-point baseline, however, it is obvious that this decreasing trend is nothing more than an artifact of having observed through this window of 10 data points a relatively small local section of the longer time series. The apparent trend is nothing more than a manifestation of random variability about a mean of 30.

Similarly, the seven-data point baseline in Figure 5.6 shows a clear increasing trend. However, as can be seen in Figure 5.4, this data pattern is, again, nothing more than a local section of the longer time series viewed through a particular seven-point window. The increasing trend is nothing more than an illusion that is the result of overinterpretation of random variation in the longer time series.

Figure 5.7 shows another possible baseline, this one having five data points, that could result from viewing the identified local section of the time series in Figure 5.4 through a window five data points wide. The apparent decreasing trend is, in this case, statistically significant. However, it is nothing more than a manifestation of random variability in the longer time series. In this case, the temptation could be to

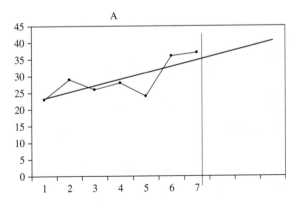

Figure 5.6 A possible baseline of seven data points pulled from the 50-point baseline in Figure 5.4. Solid line through data points is ordinary least squares (OLS) baseline trend.

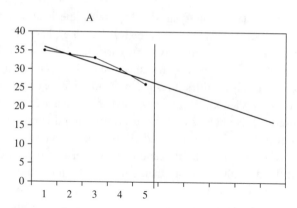

Figure 5.7 A possible baseline of five data points pulled from the 50-point baseline in Figure 5.4. Solid line through data points is ordinary least squares (OLS) baseline trend.

infer not only a decreasing trend but also one that is statistically significant.

Figure 5.8 shows one of many possible four-data point baseline phases that could be obtained from the time series in Figure 5.4. In this case, there is an apparent increasing OLS trend, with little variability about the OLS trend line. However, as the other trends are that are in Figures 5.5 through 5.7, this trend is nothing more than a

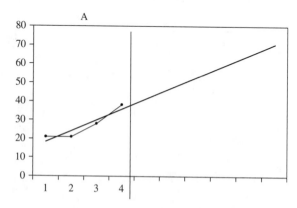

Figure 5.8 A possible baseline of four data points pulled from the 50-point baseline in Figure 5.4. Solid line through data points is ordinary least squares (OLS) baseline trend.

manifestation of random variability in the data points in the longer time series.

The important point here is, as was made in the first chapter, that every short time series in a single case design can, in principle, be viewed as a local piece of a longer time series viewed through a temporal window that allows the analyst to see only a small number of data points. Even a relatively large baseline of 10 data points, with a clear trend, can be an invitation to misinterpret random variation in a longer, stable time series with no trend. The various baselines seen in the previous figures, some with increasing trends and others with decreasing trends, all illustrate the invitation to misinterpret random variation as meaningful trend.

Now let's extend this illustration into the context of an entire AB single case design. Again consider the 10-data point baseline phase from Figure 5.5 shown in the context of the same 50-data point time series but illustrated as in Figure 5.9. This baseline phase is now followed by an equally long 10-data point "treatment phase" that is made up of the 10 points that follow the 10 "baseline" points in the 50-data point time series from Figure 5.4. This is shown as Figure 5.9. This hypothetical AB single case design is shown in the context of the entire 50-data point time series

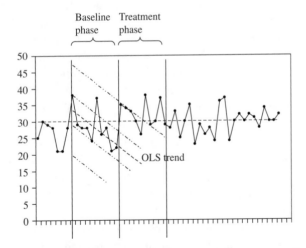

Figure 5.9 Figure 5.4 with local trend modeled as in a 10-data point baseline phase followed by a 10-data point treatment phase. The baseline phase ordinary least squares (OLS) trend line is marked and extended into and across the treatment phase. Dashed lines parallel to OLS trend line are one and three sigma bands.

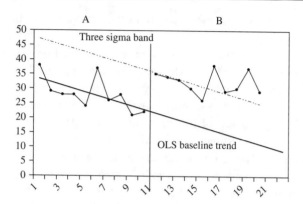

Figure 5.10 One possible AB design abstracted from data in Figure 5.6, with ordinary least squares (OLS) linear baseline trend and upper limit of three sigma band region of baseline phase background variability drawn in.

in Figure 5.4, along with an OLS linear baseline trend line and both one and three sigma band lines for "baseline phase" background variability that are extended into the "treatment" phase. The estimated baseline trend, −1.2, approaches statistical significance [$t(8) = -2.28$, $p = 0.052$]. These hypothetical AB single case design data, abstracted from this 50-data point time series, are shown in Figure 5.10 along with the extended OLS baseline phase trend line and the upper limit of the three sigma band relative to this trend line. Note that 5 of the 10 treatment phase data points fall above this three sigma band, and all 10 are on the same side of the extended trend line. Using the decision rules in Chapter 3, these patterns would be suggestive of change. If the modified decision rules stated earlier in this chapter were used, a relatively strong case could still be made for change on the basis of rule number four. Yet, this apparent change is nothing more than a manifestation of random variation in a longer time series. The data patterns seen in Figures 5.10 are, again, nothing more than an invitation to misinterpret random variation—noise—as meaningful patterns, or as signal.

This demonstration is a re-emphasis of the points made in the first chapter that the role of chance must not be underestimated when analyzing the brief time series data found in single case designs. This is also an illustration of how a misspecified baseline phase model—in this case a trend-based model—can collude with small numbers of

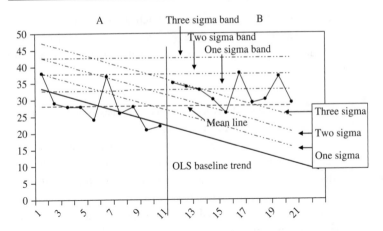

Figure 5.11 Hypothetical AB single case design data from Figure 5.9, with baseline data modeled using both mean-based and trend-based representations of background variability and associated three sigma bands.

observations to invite the analyst to misinterpret random variation as meaningful data patterns.

Now consider Figure 5.11. The data in this figure are the same as those from Figure 5.10, but with *both trend- and mean-based baseline models represented.* An extended mean line can be seen in this figure, along with the extended OLS trend line, as can the upper limits of one, two, and three sigma bands relative to both the extended OLS trend line and the extended baseline phase mean line. While the data relative to the trend-based model imply change across the AB phase transition, as noted previously, the data relative to the baseline mean-based model are far less suggestive. None of the data points fall outside of the three sigma band, and only one falls above the two sigma band, although more than eight of the treatment phase data points fall above the extended baseline phase mean line. If the analyst were to require (*1*) a conservative criterion, say, use of the three sigma rule number one from Chapter 3, or the revised version of this rule stated earlier in this chapter, and (*2*) that the results from both trend and no-trend models must converge on the same conclusion in order to infer change, then the graphics in Figure 5.11 would lead the analyst to conclude that no significant change has occurred across the AB phase single case design.

If the analyst were in a context in which a balance of type I and type II errors was important, then less conservatively, but with greater potential statistical power, the analyst could note that the results are conditional:

(1) If a trend-based model is appropriate, then there is relatively strong evidence of change across the two phases; but

(2) If the baseline trend is nothing more than a manifestation of random variation about a constant baseline mean level of the dependent variable, so a mean-based model is appropriate, then the treatment phase data pattern relative to the extended mean line and region of background variability is much less suggestive of change across the two phases.

This demonstration clearly implies that the analysis of single case design data should simultaneously make use of mean (or median)-based, and trend-based, representations of baseline data and associated background variability as a methodology to counter the seductive invitation to interpret random variation as meaningful data patterns.

EMPHASIZING "MISSING DATA" IN SINGLE CASE DESIGNS

Figure 5.12 presents again Figure 2.33, which presents the data from Figure 1.2 but with month-long baseline and treatment phases and with the data *not* obtained during 3-week-long portions of the baseline and treatment represented as "missing" data. This is not how single case design data are typically represented graphically. However, representing single case data in this manner helps the analyst, as well as the consumer of the single case design graph, to interpret the data in the context of the notion that, in principle, more data could have been obtained but were not and that the data represent a short time series abstracted from a much longer time series. This is one way to contextualize the analysis of the short time series into a frame facilitating the recognition of the risks associated with interpreting data patterns in short time series outside of the context of the longer series of which they are a part.

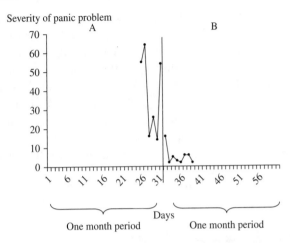

Figure 5.12 Figure 1.2 shown again, as in Figure 2.33, with time periods in baseline and treatment phases during which data were not obtained, represented in order to emphasize the amount of data *not* obtained, and hence "missing," in the short single case design time series.

RECOMMENDED CHANGES TO VISUAL ANALYSIS PROCEDURES

The visual analysis of single case design data sans any of the graphic aids discussed previously is arguably based on implicit assumptions and some form of statistical model of baseline phase data, albeit in this case a (most likely) vague and unarticulated model. The analyst himself or herself may not be aware of the assumptions and statistical model upon which the analysis he or she is conducting are based, and the reader of an article or report of this analysis is even more likely to be uninformed as to the assumptions and implicit statistical model upon which the analysis was based.

Research, using *think aloud methodologies*, investigating the thought processes used by researchers visually analyzing single case design data is now beginning to appear (e.g., Austin & Mawhinney, 1999; Wallander, 2004). In these studies, persons analyzing the data from single case designs talk out loud as they conduct the data analysis, with their verbally articulated thoughts recorded. Their verbal comments are then analyzed for information on how they think about the data and make their inferences.

Such a "think aloud" strategy could easily be used as a routine part of the analysis procedure when visually analyzing single case design data. The analyst could talk aloud as he or she conducts the data analysis, and then raters could independently code the verbiage for content concerning assumptions being made and the form of implicit statistical model the visual analyst is using. These ratings could be reported, along with interrater agreement indices, as an element of the results section of an article reporting the results of the single case design study. This information could help the consumer of the research to better assess the data analysis that was conducted.

FINAL RECOMMENDATIONS

If a single case design entails a long time series, then the methods described in Chapter 2 should be used. In such an analysis the regression-discontinuity methods could model the single case data, and the patterns of autocorrelation in the residuals would be modeled using ARIMA methods. These approaches should not be used, however, with smaller time series. It is clearly risky to arbitrarily make rules of thumb about required numbers of observations. Having said that, and recognizing that the author is making a somewhat arbitrary guideline, a minimum of 25 observations per phase, or a total of 50 for a simple AB design, would seem a reasonable minimum number required in order to employ the statistical methods in Chapter 2. These numbers would enable the analyst to assess autocorrelation functions across about 12 to 13 lags for the residuals from a statistical model applied to a total of 50 observations. This minimum number per phase would also allow the analyst to consider, with reasonable power, the role that chance might be playing in the observed time series.

In cases of shorter time series, the combined graphical and statistical methods described in Chapter 3 seem to offer a number of advantages. First, formal tests of statistical significance are not used, and that should be seen as an advantage. Tests of statistical significance have the potential to be overrelied upon for making inferences about change (Carver, 1978; Chow, 1996). Tests of statistical significance will also suffer from low statistical power when the numbers of observations are small in a time series, and it will be difficult to adequately test the assumptions upon which any statistical tests are based.

The simultaneous use of mean (or median)-based, and linear trend-based, models of baseline data, along with one, two, and three sigma bands to represent baseline phase background variability, should be employed. The graphic representations of baseline data should be extended into and across treatment phase data, and then the modified decision rules stated earlier in this chapter used. In the context of scientific research, type I error control should be paramount and, hence, in this author's view the modified three sigma rule, stated earlier in this chapter, should be used. The analyst should require the convergence of results from both mean (median)-based and trend-based representations of baseline phase data. In other words, the treatment phase data should simultaneously exceed the three sigma rule (rule number 1) stated previously *for both mean (median)- and trend-based baseline phase models*. While some have argued that SPC methods are not appropriate for detecting "unusual" human events (e.g., Borckardt et al., 2006), the three sigma rule may be a robust and conservative criterion even in the context of the small numbers of observations in short time series and the presence of autocorrelation (Wheeler, 1995).

The analyst should not only provide evidence for change in the form of descriptions of how treatment phase data contrast with baseline data patterns and how these contrasts suggest change relative to background variability, but also obtain collateral evidence, both quantitative and qualitative, that is used to consider and rule out alternative explanations for the observed data patterns, including the possibility that any baseline trend is nothing more than chance/random variability (Ostrom, 1990). Multiple models should be used as a part of the process of considering alternative explanations.

In the context of practice or program evaluation, it will be more important to balance type I and type II error control. The three sigma rule is, in the author's opinion, too stringent in this context, so depending on the degree to which the analyst wants to emphasize control over type II error, any of the modified decision rules two through four, stated earlier in this chapter, should be used, either singly or in combination depending on how many data points are in the treatment phase. However, the requirement of the convergence of results from the simultaneous use of mean (median)- and trend-based models of baseline phase data is not too conservative and should be used in the practice evaluation and program evaluation context. If the results of the analysis depend on whether the baseline data are viewed as trending or not, then, unless collateral information can be used to make a compelling case that either the no-trend or trend based model is the one that best fits the data and the results based on the best-fitting model are suggestive of change, the possibility that random variability is misleading the analyst must be considered a plausible hypothesis. Even in the practice evaluation or program evaluation context the analyst should use multiple models, both no-trend and trend-based, and require convergence of results from the different approaches unless compelling collateral evidence comes down on the side of one particular model.

Finally, if the analyst elects to eschew any form of graphical or statistical methodology and to rely instead on a purely visual analysis, then he or she should use a think-aloud procedure and audio-record his or her analysis of the single case design data. This recording should then be rated independently by at least two raters, with interrater agreement indices reported, in terms of the implicit assumptions being made by the analyst concerning the data. These assumptions would then be reported as a part of the write-up of the analysis of the data from the single case design. There will be, of course, cases in which this procedure would be less important. This would include circumstances in which the data are so compelling to imply change between phases that there can be little concern that implicit and unstated assumptions have overly and negatively influenced the analysis. The data in Figure 1.5 is one such circumstance. In cases in which the data are less compelling, however, the information provided by the think-aloud methodology could be invaluable in helping to validly interpret and understand the results of a purely visual data analysis.

FINAL CAVEAT

One final caveat is in order. The most important principle undergirding the analysis of data from single case designs is that of critical thinking. Regardless of the procedures used to analyze the data, the analyst must think critically and (1) avoid the use of any of the procedures in this book, or any other book, in a mechanical way; (2) seek and make use of collateral information, both quantitative and qualitative, to augment the single case design time series data; (3) consider alternative possibilities and explanations; and (4) avoid the temptation to fall prey to confirmation bias. This latter recommendation means the analyst must look for evidence contrary to the conclusions that he or she is tending toward as a consequence of the analysis he or she is doing. The most important analysis tool the analyst has is his or her critical thinking faculties. These should always be used.

Glossary

AB design A single system design in which a baseline phase is followed by a treatment phase (see Chapter 1, including Figure 1.2). This has been called by some the "basic single system design."

ABAB design A single system design in which a baseline phase is followed by a treatment phase, which is then followed by a second baseline phase during which the treatment or intervention in place during the treatment phase is withdrawn. There then follows a second treatment phase in which the treatment or intervention is again implemented. This is one of the stronger single case designs in terms of internal validity (see Chapter 1, including Figure 1.5).

Alternating treatments design A single case design in which two treatments are implemented at different points in time, sometimes with the differential implementation conducted in a random manner. The relative effectiveness of the treatments is then studied by connecting the observations of the dependent variable made during the implementation of one of the interventions and comparing the resulting time series against that formed by connecting the observations made during the implementation of the second of the interventions (see Chapter 1, including Figure 1.8).

ARIMA model A form of time series analysis, or time series model, called autoregressive integrated moving average (see Chapter 2, as well as McCain & McCleary, 1979).

Autocorrelation Refers to the correlation sometimes found between observations in a time series (see Chapter 2). Autocorrelation can take the form of autoregressive, moving average, or mixed autoregressive and moving average. Autocorrelation can be considered from two perspectives: within the repeated measures of the dependent variable or with the residuals from fitting some statistical model to the time series data (see Chapter 3, and especially McCain & McCleary, 1979).

Autoregressive model A time series model in which an observation of the dependent variable at a time t is influenced by—that is, correlated with—the dependent variable at one or more previous points in time. In a lag-1 autoregressive model, the observation at time t is influenced by the observation at time $t–1$; in a lag-2 model, the observation at time t is influenced by the observations at times $t–1$ and $t–2$; an so forth for lags 3 and higher (see Chapter 2, and McCain & McCleary, 1979).

Autoregressive parameter A correlation-like term that represents quantitatively the degree to which an observation at time t in a time series is influenced by the value of an observation at a previous point in the time series (see Chapter 2, and McCain & McCleary, 1979).

Baseline phase A set of measures taken of a dependent variable prior to, or after the cessation of, an intervention. Its purpose is to obtain a profile of the dependent variable in the absence of any treatment or intervention intended to change the dependent variable. A baseline can be *concurrent*, meaning the observations are made in the here and now—the present—or *retrospective*, meaning the observations are made in the past via memory (see Chapter 1, including Figures 1.1 [illustrative baseline phase] and 1.8 [example of retrospective baseline]).

B design A single system design in which repeated measures of a dependent variable are made during the application of an intervention or treatment intended to change the dependent variable. In this design no measures are taken of the dependent variable prior to or in the absence of the implementation of the intervention (see Chapter 1, including Figure 1.3). This single case design is most congenial with service provision.

B1-B2-B1-B2 design A single case deign in which one treatment is compared against another. One intervention or treatment is implemented during the first B1 phase, followed by the cessation of that treatment and the implementation of a different treatment during the first B2 phase. Then the second treatment is stopped and the first reinstated during the second B1 phase. This first treatment is then again stopped and the second intervention reimplemented during the second B2 phase (see Chapter 1, including Figure 1.6).

Interquartile range   One of several measures of dispersion. It is a measure of the degree to which a set of scores varies. It is defined as the difference between the first and third quartile scores (see Chapter 3, and Pagano, 2006).

Mean   One of three measures of central tendency. It is usually referred to as the "average."

Median   One of three measures of central tendency. It is defined as the 50th percentile score—that is, the score at which 50% of all other scores are lower (higher).

Moving average model   A time series model in which an observation of the dependent variable at a time t is influenced by—that is, correlated with—the random shock (see later) at one or more previous points in time. In a lag-1 moving average model, the observation at time t is influenced by the random shock at time t–1; in a lag-2 moving average model, the observation at time t is influenced by the random shocks at times t–1 and t–2; an so forth (see Chapter 2, and McCain & McCleary, 1979).

Moving average parameter   A correlation-like term that represents quantitatively the degree to which an observation at time t in a time series is influenced by the value of a random shock (disturbance) at a previous point in the time series (see Chapter 2, and McCain & McCleary, 1979).

Multiple baseline design   A single case design that can be thought of as a stack, or sequence, of AB designs in which each succeeding AB design in the stack, or sequence, has a systematically longer baseline phase. The multiple baseline design can be across persons, systems, or behaviors (see Chapter 1, including Figure 1.7).

Overlap   The degree to which the range of values of a dependent variable in one phase of a single case design covers or overlies the range of values in an adjacent phase. The overlap can be assessed using variability relative to a mean line or a trend line (see Chapter 3).

Random disturbance, or random shock   A term or component of an ARIMA statistical model that is analogous to the residual, or "error," term in a regression model (see Chapter 2, and McCain & McCleary, 1979).

Range   One of several indices quantifying the extent to which a set of scores varies. It is defined most often as the highest score minus the lowest score.

Region of background variability   A region or area in a graph of a single case design phase that represents the degree to which the data in the phase vary relative to some reference, such as a mean line or a trend line. This region of background variability is used as a foil against which data in an adjacent phase is compared in order to facilitate inferences concerning change, often using the notion of overlap (see Chapter 3).

Regression discontinuity model A regression model of a time series in which there is a discontinuous break in the time series, such as a sudden jump in level and/or a sudden change in trend (see Chapter 2, including Figure 2.1).

Sigma unit An index that quantifies how much the data in a time series varies. The sigma unit is used in statistical process control methodology (see Chapter 3, and Wheeler, 1995).

Single system design A research methodology that focuses on the individual person or system, such as a group, school, community, and so forth (see Chapter 1).

Standard deviation A measure of dispersion or variability. It is the square root of the variance and is another way of indicating the degree to which a set of scores varies. Technically, it is the square root of the mean squared deviation.

Stationarity A form of stability assumption made about a time series that is necessary for the use of ARIMA models (see Chapter 2, and Cromwell, Labys, & Terraza, 1993).

Time series A series of repeated observations, across a time period, of one or more variables of interest. The across-time relationship between these variables may be investigated using any of a number of methods (see, e.g., Ostrom, 1990). There may be a treatment or intervention implemented at some point during the time series with the intention of studying the impact of the treatment or intervention on the time series. A design of this type is referred to as an *interrupted time series design* (see in-depth discussion in Cook & Campbell, 1979, Chapter 5).

Treatment phase A set of measures of a dependent variable that are made while a treatment or intervention is being implemented in an effort to change the dependent variable (see Chapter 1).

Trend The rate of change of the dependent variable across a phase of a single system design. Trend can be linear or nonlinear. Usually only linear trend is represented in single system design phases. Linear trend can be represented in any of several ways (see Chapter 3).

Variance One of several measures of dispersion. It is an indicator of the degree to which a set of scores varies. Technically, it is the mean squared deviation, and is the squared standard deviation.

References

American Psychiatric Association. (1980). *Diagnostic and statistical manual of mental disorders* (3rd ed.). Washington, DC: Author.

Ascher, L. (1981). Employing paradoxical intention in the treatment of agoraphobia. *Behaviour Research and Therapy, 19*(6), 533–542.

Ash, C. (1993). *The probability tutoring book.* New York: IEEE Press.

Austin, J., & Mawhinney, T. C. (1999). Using concurrent verbal reports to examine data analyst verbal behavior. *Journal of Organizational Behavior Management, 18,* 61–81.

Baer, D. (1977). Perhaps it would be better not to know everything. *Journal of Applied Behavior Analysis, 10,* 167–172.

Bailey Jr., D. (1984). Effects of lines of progress and semilogarithmic charts on ratings of charted data. *Journal of Applied Behavior Analysis, 17,* 359–365.

Barlow, D., Hayes, S., & Nelson, R. (1984). *The scientist practitioner: Research and accountability in clinical and educational settings.* New York: Pergamon.

Barlow, D., & Hersen, M. (1984). *Single case experimental designs* (2nd ed.). New York: Pergamon.

Benbenishty, R. (1988). Combining the single-system and group approaches to evaluate treatment effectiveness on the agency level. *Journal of Social Service Research, 12,* 31–48.

Biglan, A., Ary, D., & Wagenaar, A. (2000). The value of interrupted time-series experiments for community intervention research. *Prevention Science, 1*(1), 31–49.

Bloom, M., & Fischer, J. (1982). *Evaluating practice: Guidelines for the accountable professional.* Englewood Cliffs, NJ: Prentice Hall.

Bloom, M., Fischer, J., & Orme, J. (2008). *Evaluating practice: Guidelines for the accountable professional* (6th ed.). Needham Heights, MA: Allyn & Bacon.

Borckardt, J., Pelic, C., Herbert, J., Borckardt, D., Nash, M., Cooney, H., & Hardesty, S. (2006). An autocorrelation-corrected nonparametric control chart technique for health care quality applications. *Quality Management in Health Care, 15*(3), 157–162.

Borckardt, J. J., Murphy, M. D., Nash, M. R., & Shaw, D. (2004). An empirical examination of visual analysis procedures for clinical practice evaluation. *Journal of Social Service Research, 30*(3), 55–73.

Box, G., & Jenkins, G. (1976). *Time series analysis: Forecasting and control* (rev. ed.). Oakland, CA: Holden-Day.

Box, G., Jenkins, G., & Reinsel, G. (2008). Time series analysis: Forecasting and control (4th ed.). New York: Wiley.

Box, G., & Tiao, G. (1975). Intervention analysis with applications to economic and environmental problems. *Journal of the American Statistical Association, 70,* 70–92.

Boykin, R. A., & Nelson, R. O. (1981). The effects of instructions and calculation procedures on observers' accuracy, agreement, and calculation correctness. *Journal of Applied Behavior Analysis, 14,* 479–489.

Brennan, R. (2001). *Generalizability theory.* New York: Springer.

Brossart, D., Parker, R., Olson, E., & Mahadevan, L. (2006). The relationship between visual analysis and five statistical analyses in a simple AB single-case research design. *Behavior Modification, 30,* 531–563.

Bryk, A., & Raudenbush, S. (1992). *Hierarchical linear models: Applications and data analysis methods.* Newbury Park, CA: Sage.

Bryk, A., Raudenbush, S., Seltzer, M., & Congdon, R. (1988). *An introduction to HLM: Computer program and user's guide* (2nd ed.). Chicago: University of Chicago Department of Education.

Busk, P. L., & Marascuilo, L. A. (1988). Autocorrelation in single-subject research: A counterargument to the myth of no autocorrelation. *Behavioral Assessment, 10,* 229–242.

Busk, P. L., & Marascuilo, L. A. (1992). Statistical analysis in single-case research: Issues, procedures, and recommendations, with applications to multiple behaviors. In T. R. Kratochwill & J. R. Levin (Eds.), *Single-case research design and analysis* (pp. 159–185). Hillsdale, NJ: Erlbaum.

Campbell, J. (2004). Statistical comparison of four effect sizes for single-subject designs. *Behavior Modification, 28,* 234–246.

Carver, R. (1978). The case against statistical significance testing. *Harvard Educational Review, 48*(3), 378–399.

Chow, S. (1996). *Statistical significance: Rationale, validity, and utility.* Thousand Oaks, CA: Sage.

Cohen, J., Cohen, P., West, S., & Aiken, L. (2003). *Applied multiple regression/correlation analysis for the behavioral sciences* (3rd ed.). Mahwah, NJ: Erlbaum.

Conger, J. (1956). Alcoholism: Theory, problem, and challenge. *Quarterly Journal in the Study of Alcohol, 17,* 296–305.

Cook, D., & Campbell, D. (1979). *Quasi-experimentation.* Boston: Houghton Mifflin.

Cromwell, J., Labys, W., & Terraza, M. (1993). *Univariate tests for time series models.* Thousand Oaks, CA: Sage.

Crosbie, J. (1987). The inability of the binomial test to control Type I error with single-subject data. *Behavioral Assessment, 9,* 141–150.

Crosbie, J. (1995). Interrupted time-series analysis with short series: Why it is problematic; how it can be improved. In J. M. Gottman (Ed.), *The analysis of change* (pp. 361–395). Mahwah, NJ: Erlbaum.

DeProspero, A., & Cohen, S. (1979). Inconsistent visual analysis of intrasubject data. *Journal of Applied Behavior Analysis, 12,* 573–579.

Dickey, D. A., & Fuller, W. (1979), Distribution of the estimators for autoregressive time series with a unit root. *Journal of the American Statistical Association, 74,* 427–431.

Edington, E. (1982). Non-parametric tests for single-subject multiple schedule experiments. *Behavioral Assessment, 4,* 83–91.

Ellis, R., & Gulick, D. (1986). *Calculus with analytic geometry* (3rd ed.). New York: Harcourt, Brace, Jovanovich.

Fisher, W., Kelley, M., & Lomas, J. (2003). Visual aids and structured criteria for improving visual inspection and interpretation of single-case designs. *Journal of Applied Behavior Analysis, 36,* 387–406.

Foa, E. (1979). Failure in treating obsessive-compulsives. *Behaviour Research & Therapy, 17,* 169–176.

Foa, E., Grayson, J., Steketee, G., Doppelt, H., Turner, R., & Latimer, P. (1983). Success and failure in the behavioral treatment of obsessive-compulsives. *Journal of Consulting and Clinical Psychology, 15,* 287–297.

Franklin, R. D., Gorman, B. S., Beasley, T. M., & Allison, D. B. (1996). Graphical display and visual analysis. In R. D. Franklin, D. B. Allison, & B. S. Gorman (Eds.), *Design and analysis of single case research* (pp. 119–158). Mahwah, NJ: Erlbaum.

Furlong, M., & Wampold, B. (1981). Visual analysis of single-subject studies by school psychologists. *Psychology in the Schools, 18,* 80–86.

Furlong, M., & Wampold, B. (1982). Intervention effects and relative variation as dimensions in experts' use of visual inference. *The Journal of Applied Behavior Analysis, 15*, 415–421.

Garb, H. (1998). *Studying the clinician: Judgment research and psychological assessment.* Washington, DC: American Psychological Association.

Gentile, J., Roden, A., & Klein, R. (1974). An analysis of variance model for the intrasubject replication design. *Journal of Applied Behavior Analysis, 5*, 193–198.

Gibson, G. (1988). Characteristics influencing the visual analysis of single subject data: An empirical analysis. *The Journal of Applied Behavioral Science, 24*(3), 298–314.

Gibson, G., & Ottenbacher, K. (1988). Inconsistent visual analysis of intrasubject data: An empirical analysis. *Journal of Applied Behavioral Science, 24*, 298–314.

Giere, R. (1990). *Explaining science: A cognitive approach.* Chicago: University of Chicago Press.

Gilovich, T. (1993). *How we know what isn't so.* New York: The Free Press.

Gilovich, T., Griffin, D., & Kahneman, D. (Eds.). (2002). *Heuristics and biases: The psychology of intuitive judgment.* New York: Cambridge University Press.

Gottman, J. (1981). *Time series analysis: A comprehensive introduction for social scientists.* New York: Cambridge University Press.

Gottman, J., & Leiblum, S. (1974). *How to do psychotherapy and how to evaluate it.* New York: Holt, Rinehart, and Winston.

Gresham, F., & Noell, G. (1993). Documenting the effectiveness of consultation outcomes. In J. Zims, T. Kratochwill, and S. Elliott (Eds.), *Handbook of consultation services for children: Applications in educational and clinical settings* (pp. 249–273). San Francisco, CA: Josey-Bass.

Harbst, K., Ottenbacher, K., & Harris, S. (1991). Interrater reliability of therapists judgements of graphed data. *Physical Therapy, 71*, 107–115.

Heard, K., & Watson, T. (1999). Reducing wandering by persons with dementia using differential reinforcement. *Journal of Applied Behavior Analysis, 32*, 381–384.

Hojem, M., & Ottenbacher, K. (1988). Empirical investigation of visual inspection versus trend-line analysis of single-subject data. *Journal of the American Physical Therapy Association, 68*, 983–988.

Hsen-Hsing, M. (2006). An alternative method for quantitative synthesis of single-subject researches: Percentage of data points exceeding the median. *Behavior Modification, 30*, 598–617.

Hudson, W. (1982). *The clinical measurement package.* Homewood, IL: Dorsey.

Huitema, B. (1985). Autocorrelation in behavioral research: A myth. *Behavioral Assessment, 7*, 109–120.

Huitema, B. (1986). Autocorrelation in behavioral research: Wherefore art thou? In A. Poling and R. Fuqua (Eds.), *Research methods in applied behavior analysis: Issues and advances* (pp. 187–208). New York: Plenum.

Huitema, B. E. (1988). Autocorrelation: 10 years of confusion. *Behavioral Assessment, 10,* 253–294.

Huitema, B., & McKean, J. (1998). Irrelevant autocorrelation in least-squares intervention models. *Psychological Methods, 3*(1), 104–116.

Johnson, M., & Ottenbacher, K. (1991). Trend line influence on visual analysis of single subject data in rehabilitation research. *International Disability Studies, 13*(2), 55–59.

Johnston, J., & Pennypacker, H. (1980). *Strategies and tactics of human behavioral research.* Hillsdale, NJ: Lawrence Erlbaum.

Jones, R., Weinrott, M., & Vaught, R. (1978). Effects of serial dependency on the agreement between visual and statistical inferences. *Journal of Applied Behavioral Science, 11,* 277–283.

Kazdin, A. (1981). Drawing valid inferences from case studies. *Journal of Consulting and Clinical Psychology,49,* 183–192.

Kazdin, A. (1982). *Single case research designs: Methods for clinical and applied settings.* New York: Oxford University Press.

Kazdin, A. (2003). *Research design in clinical psychology* (4th ed.). Old Tappon, NJ: Pearson.

Kratochwill, T. (1992). Single-case research design and analysis: An overview. In T. Kratochwill & J. Levin (Eds.), *Single-case research design and analysis: New directions for psychology and education* (pp. 1–14). Hillsdale, NJ: Lawrence Erlbaum.

Ma, H. (2006). An alternative method for quantitative synthesis of single subject researches. *Behavior Modification, 5,* 598–617.

Matyas, T., & Greenwood, K. (1990). Visual analysis of single-case time series: Effects of variability, serial dependency, and magnitude of intervention effects. *Journal of Applied Behavior Analysis, 23,* 341–351.

McCain, L., & McCleary, R. (1979). The statistical analysis of the simple interrupted time-series quasi-experiment. In T. Cook and D. Campbell, *Quasi-experimentation: Design & analysis issues for field settings* (pp. 233–293). Boston: Houghton-Mifflin.

McCleary, R., & Welsh, W. (1992). Philosophical and statistical foundations of time-series experiments. In T. Kratochwill & J. Levin (Eds.), *Single-case research design and analysis: New directions for psychology and education* (pp. 41–92). Hillsdale, NJ: Lawrence Erlbaum.

McDowell, D., McCleary, R., Meidinger, E., & Hay, R. (1980). *Interrupted time series analysis.* Thousand Oaks, CA: Sage.

Michael, J. (1974). Statistical inference for individual organism research: Mixed blessing or curse? *Journal of Applied Behavior Analysis, 7,* 647–653.

Neter, J., Wasserman, W., & Kutner, M. (1983). *Applied linear regression models.* Homewood, IL: Richard D. Irwin, Inc.

Normand, M., & Bailey, J. (2006). The effects of celebration lines on visual data analysis. *Behavior Analysis, 30,* 412–423.

Nourbakhsh, M., & Ottenbacher, K. (1994). The statistical analysis of single-subject data: A comparative examination. *Physical Therapy, 74*(8), 768–776.

Nugent, W. (1987). Information gain through integrated research approaches. *Social Service Review, 61,* 337–364.

Nugent, W. (1992). The affective impact of a clinical social worker's interviewing style: A series of single case experiments. *Research on Social Work Practice, 2*(1), 6–27.

Nugent, W. (1993). A series of single case design clinical evaluations of an Ericksonian hypnotic intervention used with clinical anxiety. *Journal of Social Service Research, 17*(3/4), 41–69.

Nugent, W. (1996). Integrating single-case and group-comparison designs for evaluation research. *Journal of Applied Behavioral Science, 32*(2), 209–226.

Nugent, W. (2000). Single case design visual analysis procedures for use in practice evaluation. *Journal of Social Service Research, 27*(2), 39–76.

Nugent, W., Champlin, D., & Wiinimaki, L. (1997). The effects of anger control training on adolescent antisocial behavior. *Research on Social Work Practice, 7*(4), 446–462.

Nugent, W., Sieppert, J., & Hudson, W. (2001). *Practice evaluation for the 21st century.* Belmont, CA: Wadsworth.

Orme, J., & Cox, M. E. (2001). Analyzing single-subject design data using statistical process control charts. *Social Work Research, 25*(2), 115–127.

Ostrom, C. (1990). *Time series analysis: Regression techniques* (2nd ed.). Beverly Hills, CA: Sage.

Ottenbacher, K. (1990). Visual analysis of single-subject data: An empirical analysis. *Mental Retardation, 28,* 283–290.

Ottenbacher, K., & Cusick, A. (1991). An empirical investigation of interrater agreement for single-subject data using graphs with and without trend lines. *Journal of the Association for Persons with Severe Handicaps, 16,* 48–55.

Pagano, R. (2006). *Understanding statistics in the behavioral sciences* (8th ed.). Belmont, CA: Wadsworth.

Parker, R., & Hagan-Burke, S. (2007). Median based overlap analysis for single-case data: A second study. *Behavior Modification, 31,* 919–936.

Parsonson, B., & Baer, D. (1986). The graphic analysis of data. In A. Poling & R. Fuqua (Eds.), *Research methods in applied behavior analysis: Issues and advances* (pp. 157–186). New York: Plenum.

Parsonson, B., & Baer, D. (1992). The visual analysis of data, and current research into the stimuli controlling it. In T. Kratochwill & J. Levin (Eds.), *Single-case research design and analysis: New directions for psychology and education* (pp. 15–40). Hillsdale, NJ: Lawrence Erlbaum.

Pfadt, A., Cohen, I., Sudhalter, V., Romanczyk, R., & Wheeler, D. (1992). Applying statistical process control to clinical data: An illustration. *Journal of Applied Behavior Analysis, 25*(3), 551–560.

Pfadt, A., & Wheeler, D. (1995). Using statistical process control to make data-based clinical decisions. *Journal of Applied Behavior Analysis, 28,* 349–370.

Plous, S. (1993). *The psychology of judgment and decision making.* New York: McGraw-Hill.

Rogosa, D., Brand, D., & Zimowski, M. (1982). A growth curve approach to the measurement of change. *Psychological Bulletin, 90,* 726–748.

Rogosa, D., & Willett, B. (1985). Understanding correlates of change by modeling individual differences in growth. *Psychometika, 50,* 203–228.

Rojahn, J., & Schulze, H. H. (1985). The linear regression line as a judgmental aid in visual analysis of serially dependent A-B time-series data. *Journal of Psychopathology & Behavioral Assessment, 7,* 191–206.

Rubin, A., & Babbie, E. (2007). *Research methods for social work* (6th ed.). Boston: Brooks-Cole.

Rubin, A., & Knox, K. (1996). Data analysis problems in single-case evaluations: Issues for research on social work practice. *Research on Social Work Practice, 6,* 40–65.

Scruggs, T., & Mastropieri, M. (1998). Summarizing single subject research. *Behavior Modification, 3,* 221–242.

Sidman, M. (1960). *Tactics of scientific research.* New York: Basic Books.

Spiegler, M., & Guevremont, D. (2003). *Contemporary behavior therapy* (4th ed.). Belmont, CA: Wadsworth.

Stocks, T., & Williams, M. (1995). Evaluation of single-subject data using statistical hypothesis tests versus visual inspection of charts with and without celeration lines. *Journal of Social Service Research, 20,* 105–127.

Thyer, B., & Curtis, G. (1984). The effects of ethanol intoxication on phobic anxiety. *Behaviour Research and Therapy, 22,* 599–610.

Tryon, W. (1982). A simplified time-series analysis for evaluating treatment interventions. *Journal of Applied Behavior Analysis, 15,* 423–429.

Wallander, R. (2004). Employing protocol analysis in the study of visual interpretation of functional analysis data. Dissertation, University of Tennessee, Knoxville, TN.

Ware, J. (1985). Linear models for the analysis of longitudinal studies. *American Statistician, 39,* 95–101.

Wheeler, D. (1995). *Advanced topics in statistical process control.* Knoxville, TN: SPC Press.

Wheeler, D., & Chambers, D. (1992). *Understanding statistical process control* (2nd ed.). Knoxville, TN: SPC Press.

White, O., & Haring, N. (1980). *Exceptional teaching* (2nd ed.). Columbus, OH: Charles E. Merrill.

Willett, J., Ayoub, C., & Robinson, D. (1991). Using growth curve modeling to examine systematic differences in growth: An example of change in the functioning of families at risk of maladaptive parenting, child abuse, or neglect. *Journal of Consulting and Clinical Psychology, 59,* 38–47.

Wolery, M., & Billingsley, F. (1982). An application of Revusky's Rn test to slope and level changes. *Behavioral Assessment, 4,* 93–103.

Wolpe, J. (1973). *The practice of behavior therapy.* New York: Pergamon.

Woodall, W. H. (2000). Controversies and contradictions in statistical process control. *Journal of Quality Technology, 32*(4), 341–350.

Index